T2
TRAINSPOTTING

W0007528

T2
TRAINSPOTTING

John Hodge

Based on the books
PORNO *and* TRAINSPOTTING
by Irvine Welsh

FABER & FABER

First published in 2017
by Faber & Faber Limited
Bloomsbury House
74–77 Great Russell Street
London WC1B 3DA

Typeset by Country Setting, Kingsdown, Kent CT14 8ES
Printed and bound in the UK by CPI Group (UK) Ltd, Croydon CR0 4YY

A CIP record for this book
is available from the British Library

ISBN 978–0–571–33836–8

FSC
www.fsc.org
MIX
Paper from
responsible sources
FSC® C020471

2 4 6 8 10 9 7 5 3 1

CONTENTS

INTRODUCTION

What happens? That was the question that made me panic slightly, the one for which I had no answer.

I had my excuses ready. Danny had instigated this trip to Edinburgh in May 2014, along with producers Andrew Macdonald and Christian Colson, and with the promise of Irvine Welsh in town when we got there. This was to be the week we would kick-start the development of a follow-up to *Trainspotting*. In my mind, however, this was to be a few days of sightseeing, at the producers' expense, during which the impossibility of the task would become clear to everyone. The script, most likely, would never be finished and no one would be surprised. No drama, no fuss, just a gentle fade-out at the end of which (maybe months later) I would declare that I had been unable to complete a draft. Not because I didn't want to. Everyone wants to work. I just had no idea what would happen in the actual story.

Irvine's follow-up, *Porno* (2002), offered certain key pillars for the narrative – Begbie in gaol, Simon running a pub but dreaming of vice, Renton in exile, Spud much as ever – but that was more than a decade earlier, and besides, I felt there was a divergence in the *Trainspotting* world. On the one hand, there was the journey that Irvine himself had lead his creations on, the true path I suppose, and then there was the route followed by the characters in the 1996 film, similar to their cousins on the true path but undoubtedly distinct from them. Those characters, Irvine's inventions refracted through script, direction and performance into something slightly different, would not – I felt – dovetail with the detail of his novel. But I had no idea what to replace that with.

In addition I was troubled by the question of *why*? The simple answer is: to make a film, to collect a fee. But that will only get you in the chair, it won't put words on the page. Who are these people? What are they doing? Why am I watching? These questions, which are really just one, baffled me. The old expression is writer's block, but I have never heard anyone admit to suffering from that.

Conversations about making a follow-up to *Trainspotting* had occurred sporadically over the years, and I had even written a draft in the early 2000s, after the publication of *Porno*, but the script was no good and the time was not right, and after that I felt it was buried forever.

Two and half years ago, however, Danny evidently decided this was not how it would be left. Declaring that this was the last opportunity to revisit the characters whom we loved, he contacted our four leading actors, all of whom expressed an interest in principle, or at least did not dismiss it out of hand, and armed with that he insisted that we must now go to Edinburgh and there, inspired by our surroundings, we would thrash this out once and for all.

Well, who doesn't love a trip to Edinburgh, and it's not for me to go around shattering the illusions of decent people, so I got on the train and I tried to look positive about the whole pointless, doomed enterprise. And, you will be glad to know, I had a very nice time, completely untroubled by any sense of obligation or creative pressure. The journey was good, we stayed in a very pleasant flat in the old town, ate well, met lots of interesting people, talked about the film in an enjoyably vague and hypothetical fashion, and generally did what you might expect of film-makers on a jolly. And all the while I'm thinking: *this is going exactly according to plan.* No one, I thought, would consider this to be significant progress. The nut has not been cracked, the knot remains uncut. The relief! No one can claim to be let down when it comes to nothing and we all move on with our lives.

On the last full day – in a lull between the lulls – Andrew, Danny and I, like a trio of decadent boulevardiers, decided to go and see a film, at the Cameo, near Tollcross. Arriving at the cinema well in advance of the screening, we opted to have coffee in the bar there. I think I had a pastry with mine. It was that kind of afternoon. Then Danny drew my attention to something he had noticed on the wall, which was covered with photographs of various actors and directors who had visited the cinema over the years. *There*, he said, *there we are.* And sure enough, there was the image of the two of us, from eighteen years earlier, on the opening night of *Trainspotting*, when we had introduced the film at the Cameo. Eighteen years younger, staring out, slightly startled by the flash. We hadn't expected that. We finished our coffee and went to watch the film.

The following afternoon, as we went our separate ways from the platform at King's Cross, I did my best to lower expectations, promising only to see what I could do.

So about four months later, having written almost nothing, and still expecting to shortly give up, still wondering what happens and why, I was surprised when, one random afternoon, a feeling, and a tone, started to form in my mind, and with that came a rhythm, a few lines here and there, the bones of a structure. And I think it was that moment in the Cameo, really, that sense of *coming back*, that unlocked the script for me. And following on from this, the characters (Irvine's characters, the actors' characters) began to talk in my head, and once that starts, they do all the work for you. And that question of *why?* that had troubled me before, I think the script (or the film) is the answer in itself.

What happens, I had asked myself. What happens, it turns out, is what happens.

John Hodge
December 2016

CAST AND CREW

TRISTAR PICTURES

and

FILM 4

Present

In association with Creative Scotland

A DNA Films   Decibel Films
Cloud Eight Films Production

A Danny Boyle Film

T2 TRAINSPOTTING

PRINCIPAL CAST

RENTON	Ewan McGregor
SPUD	Ewen Bremner
BEGBIE	Robert Carlyle
and	
SICK BOY	Jonny Lee Miller

PRINCIPAL CREW

Directed by	Danny Boyle
Written by	John Hodge
Based on the books	
Porno *and* Trainspotting *by*	Irvine Welsh
Produced by	Andrew Macdonald
	Danny Boyle
	Christian Colson
	Bernard Bellew
Executive Producers	Irvine Welsh
	Allon Reich
Director of Photography	Anthony Dod Mantle

Production Designers	Mark Tildesley
	Patrick Rolfe
Editor	Jon Harris
Original Music by	Rick Smith
Costume Designers	Rachael Fleming
	Steven Noble
Hair and Makeup Designer	Ivana Primorac
Visual Effects Supervisor	Adam Gascoyne
Sound Designer	Glenn Freemantle
Production Sound Mixer	Colin Nicolson
Casting by	Gail Stevens

T2 TRAINSPOTTING
was first released in the United Kingdom
on 27 January 2017

T2
Trainspotting

INT. GYM. DAY

A black matt surface. It starts moving, slowly at first.

It is the rubber treadmill of a running machine.

A pair of male feet in trainers step on and start walking.

The pace increases steadily, then the machine tilts to create a gradient.

The feet keep pace, soon running at several kilometres per hour.

The runner is Mark Renton: he looks lean, fit and healthy in middle age. A regular, perhaps obsessive, exerciser.

There are other running machines, other runners, a line of them, but we are only interested in him. There may be some signage in Dutch, some ambient conversation in that language, soon drowned out by the thud of his footsteps.

While he runs, brief images flash past:

Buildings from the Dutch Republic's golden age.

Rembrandt's paintings.

Canals, dykes, bicycles, trams, tourists, coffee houses, great footballers, Anne Frank, Theo van Gogh, football hooligans, etc.

He sips from a cup of water. Wipes his face with a clean white towel.

On the running machine, the speed and gradient continue to increase.

Renton is connected to a heart monitor which shows his heart rate on the display in front of him: 130 . . . 140 . . . 150 . . . 160 . . . 165 . . .

His feet are pounding the rubber. Running as fast as he can. He's sweating, breathing heavily but determined to keep going . . .

168 . . . 170 . . . 171 . . . 173 . . .

Then without warning:

Renton's hand slaps the red emergency stop button. An ugly fall, over before we can even register that it is happening. His legs buckling like he's been shot. His already unconscious body slapping down, limbs askew, awkwardly on to the suddenly slowing treadmill. His head flopping back on to a hard edge with a nasty crack, eyes wide and vacant.

EXT. OLD TRAMSHED. DAY

Titles over:

Super-8 footage.

Young boys playing, ages five to seven. The mid-1970s. A semi-derelict old tram depot, crumbling brickwork, concrete surface.

There are a dozen or more boys playing football, but four on whom we concentrate, four who resemble the protagonists of this story, revisited in childish moments that foretell their future, then captured in freeze frame.

There might be little girls there too, elusive, wary, scornful.

Gradually the picture and music fade out to darkness and silence.

MAIN TITLE

Audio: the sound of a prison door.

INT. SAUGHTON PRISON. DAY

A modern prison.

A block. Single-storey. About ten doors down either side. Fixed tables and chairs in the centre of the space. Guard's station with desk etc. just inside the door.

A man is being escorted through the prison by two Prison Officers on his way to an appointment.

All others in the wing are in their cells. We can hear a few shouts. Radios playing.

At the frequent steel doors, they pause for the turning of locks. Walk . . .

*door . . . walk . . . door . . . then continue until they reach the
administrative area of the prison.*

The man is Frank Begbie.

They reach an interview room. His lawyer, Stoddart, is waiting inside.

He stands to welcome Begbie.

*As the Prison Officers close the door, one nods a coded message to
Stoddart: we're outside if you need us.*

INT. PRISON INTERVIEW ROOM. DAY

*They sit. Facing one another across a table. The lawyer with his back
to the door, Begbie with his to the wall.*

Stoddart breaks the silence.

STODDART

I'm afraid it's a 'no', Frank.

BEGBIE

Oh.

He visibly controls himself.

*Stoddart's hand drifts – just in case – under the table towards a yellow
panic button located on the underside of the edge.*

BEGBIE

Well, well, well . . . that is a body blow, I can tell you.

STODDART

I am sorry.

BEGBIE

Yes. A blow. No two ways about that.

*He forces a brave smile. But his composure starts to unravel from
here on.*

BEGBIE

Five more years to go.

STODDART

Yes, I know, Frank, it's a hard road.

BEGBIE

What do they think I am? Am I like one of they cunts in
the Bible that lives for ever? Is that it? Is that what they
think ah am?

STODDART

I'm not sure . . . they make an assessment –

BEGBIE

Ah've wrote letters, you know. Letters to every cunt. Tae
the Queen.

STODDART

You've written to the Queen?

BEGBIE

Aye. Nivir got back tae us, likes. Too busy to speak to
the working classes. Of course, when she needs a soldier,
it's a different story – step this way, Mr Begbie, sign here,
Mr Begbie.

STODDART

I didn't know you had served in the army?

BEGBIE

Ah huvnae. How could I? I've been in the fucking jail for
twenty year. Or did you not notice?

STODDART

Of course.

BEGBIE

Diminished responsibility.

*Stoddart's heart sinks. That is the phrase he was desperately hoping
not to hear. There's a question looming that he has to avoid.*

If that cunt at the original trial had put in a proper defence
of diminished responsibility, I would have walked out the
door a free man.

STODDART

Who's to say, Frank? Who's to say what might have been.

Aye, aye, who's to say.

Stoddart mistakenly thinks that Begbie may be mollified. Thinks he's got away with it.

STODDART

I think for you that the best policy now is to focus on . . .
staying . . . clear of situations where you may find yourself –

BEGBIE

Did you mention it?

Stoddart stops in his tracks.

BEGBIE

The diminished responsibility. Did you mention it?

Oh, no.

STODDART

At the . . . hearing?

BEGBIE

Aye. Did you?

STODDART

I . . . I felt it was more constructive –

BEGBIE

You didnae fucking mention it.

STODDART

Mr Begbie, as your solicitor, it is important that my
professional judgement –

BEGBIE

Didnae fucking mention it. Cannae believe that. What did
I say to you last time? What did I say to you? 'Mind and tell
them about the diminished responsibility.'

STODDART

I think it would be better if we brought this meeting to a
close, and you and I get together when you have had time
to reflect upon the situation.

A tense silence.

Begbie stares him in the eye.

Stoddart gulps. His hand is drifting under the table again. He freezes.

Stand-off.

BEGBIE

So: you gaunae press that wee yellow button or no?

A dilemma. Pressing the button will rescue Stoddart, but it will also be the final provocation for Begbie. Not pressing it, on the other hand, offers no absolute certainty of a peaceful ending.

Eye to eye. Who will move first? Suddenly – both at once –

Stoddart presses the button – loud bell rings.

Begbie lurches over the table, grasping the lawyer around the throat.

The door swings open – Prison Officers rushing in.

BEGBIE

You cuuunnt!

And the lawyer's head smashes back against the wall.

EXT. PORT SUNSHINE. DAY

A sad, lonely pub, doomed by forces of de-industrialisation, demographic change, and social fragmentation. It stands alone at the edge of wasteland.

INT. PORT SUNSHINE, BAR. DAY

Old-style 1970s boozer. Chipped formica. Plaid carpet stained homogeneous beige.

There are only two people present: Simon, aka Sick Boy, standing behind the bar, and a young woman, Veronika, who is seated at a table some distance from the bar, with a glass of water in front of her.

Neither says anything. Simon is drying a pint glass. He's probably been drying it for half an hour. The cloth squeaks across the glass, his eyes on Veronika. They are waiting for a call.

Her phone rings. She takes the call. Listens. Her eyes meet Simon's. He puts the glass down.

INT. REHAB GROUP ROOM. DAY

Spud is standing, facing his recovery group. A mixture of men and women of various ages face him in an almost complete circle of chairs.

The man beside him, Tom, is the oldest in the room, a veteran of these struggles.

SPUD

Daylight saving . . .

He sighs, looks to the faces in front of him. Oh yes, that was his downfall.

Well, me, I'm no likesay one way or the other when it comes to daylight. Neither a saver nor a spender. More, likesay, agnostic, ken. Unfortunately, it husnae shown the same ambivalence towards me.

He gathers his thoughts to tell the tale.

And as he speaks, we cut away to moments that chart his tale of woe:

– Spud at work on a construction site;

– with partner Gail and his son Fergus (at various ages to align with Spud's memory);

– on the site, losing his job for being late;

– in offices where public officials chastise him for being late;

– various analogue and digital clocks shifting by one hour;

– the arrival of summer: blue skies, ice creams, beaches;

– on a bare floor, Spud's personal winter;

– Spud in a jumper, still cold;

– a farmer in the bucolic idyll: cute lambs;

– the junky Spud in cold turkey;

– Gail and Fergus once again.

And in these places, the circle of chairs is sometimes also present, with its audience from the recovery group.

He begins brightly, aware of the entertainment of the story for his audience, but as it sinks towards its hopeless conclusion, the fun has somehow left the room.

SPUD

I had a job. Construction. Labouring. Bit of carpentry, bit of plumbing now and again. I mean it wasn't my first choice of vocation but they cats at the benefits office had made it clear. No coal, no dole, see. But . . . I'm off the skag, I'm seeing Gail and wee Fergus – well he's no so wee now but this was back then – I'm holding it together. But . . . one morning I was fired, for being an hour late. Then I'm an hour late at the DSS to explain why I lost the job. Then I'm an hour late to appeal against losing my benefits, an hour late for my work-focused interview and an hour late for my supervised visit to wee Fergus, and late again at the Social Services to explain why! Eventually, I lit on to it. Clocks gone forward. One hour. British Summer Time, they called it. Wisnae even warm: I was still wearing a jumper. They said it happens every year, well how would I know – I'd been on the skag for fifteen years and you know how it is . . . daylight is not high on your agenda when you got a habit. It's for farmers and that, dudes who have to tend to their livestock, not junkies who need to score. So that was me . . . No job, no money, no access to the wee fellow.

TOM

And you went back on the heroin.

SPUD

Aye. My friend. Only friend that's never left us.

TOM

Well, Daniel, you're among real friends here and we're glad you've come back.

Tom rests a hand on Spud's shoulder and he speaks to the group, but we stay on Spud's face, where the truth and dread of Tom's words are clear enough.

TOM

And of course, as Daniel knows, it's easy enough when you're here. Talk is easy when we're supported, surrounded by people who understand, who know how we feel.

EXT. SPUD'S BEDSIT. DAY

Spud walks home, despondent and alone.

TOM
(*voice-over*)

It's when you're at home, when you're all alone, and you're asking yourself how your life ended up like this: that's when it's a struggle, that's when it really hurts, that's when a man can find himself driven to despair.

INT. VARIOUS / EXT. VARIOUS

In moving picture now, the people seen reprimanding Spud for his lateness – employers, officials, Gail, the farmer – all turn their back on him in weary disappointment.

Gail glances back once, then turns away again.

INT. HOTEL ROOM I. NIGHT

Simon sits in a hotel room, eating while watching a laptop screen.

On the screen, a man and a young woman disrobing, fondling, engaging in foreplay. There is single camera point of view and the woman's face is not seen.

We slowly pass through the wall . . .

INT. HOTEL ROOM 2. NIGHT

. . . into the adjacent room where a clock beside the bed has a lens concealed at the centre, recording and transmitting wirelessly to the laptop next door.

The man and woman continue their activity. The woman is more in charge, confidently getting what she wants, which the man seems to enjoy. She keeps on her basque and her underwear. She never seems to face the hidden camera, though the man doesn't notice this. He's too busy enjoying himself.

The man is forty-something and his name is Tulloch. He is naked.

The woman is Veronika.

INT. HOTEL ROOM I. NIGHT

Simon continues to watch with a detached, dispassionate interest.

The half-eaten plate of food has been put aside and he chops out a line of cocaine beside the laptop which he snorts up while the sex continues inches from his eyes.

INT. HOTEL ROOM 2. NIGHT

Commandingly, her face still unseen, the young woman turns Tulloch on to his front.

She reaches for something beside the bed. Something strappy and big.

INT. HOTEL ROOM I. NIGHT

Simon nods with approval at this development.

EXT. HOTEL. NIGHT

Tulloch, now fully dressed, briefcase and raincoat, hurries from the hotel towards a parked car.

INT. CAR. NIGHT

Just as Tulloch gets into the driver's seat, the passenger door opens and Simon gets in, pulling the door shut as he does so.

                         TULLOCH
    What is this?

Simon deliberately misinterprets the question as referring to a USB drive that he holds in one hand.

SIMON

This is for you. It's a recording. A little keepsake so that the memory need never fade.

He places it into the hand of the startled Tulloch, whose world is already collapsing around him.

TULLOCH

Who are you?

SIMON

I am your blackmailer, and your salvation. If you cooperate with me, no one will ever see that video. But let's not celebrate just yet: this is not going to go away. Not like old days. No one-off payment and burn the negatives, oh no, not any more. This is a long-term relationship.

Tulloch is shaking his head, trying to say he can't but the words won't come out.

Now, my research suggests that as Deputy Headmaster of one of Edinburgh's leading private schools, you earn near enough seventy thousand pounds, per annum. It's not in my interests to squeeze you too hard and not in yours to provoke me. So let's meet in the middle. Ten per cent of your salary per annum, paid monthly, on a rolling indefinite basis.

Tulloch finds a moment of rebellion in himself. He grabs Simon by the lapel, thrusting him back against the car window.

TULLOCH

You disgusting shit! I will not stand for this!

Simon is not flustered.

SIMON

Naturally, you'll have to lie to your wife. If you need inspiration, just imagine her reaction to that. Or how much it might interest the pupils at that leading private school. I think they might enjoy the interlude with the strap-on. I know I did.

He smiles. Tulloch is broken. He release his grip on Simon.

Simon opens the door and gets out.

SIMON

I'm going to text you the details of a bank account. I expect to see a thousand-pound payment in there by the end of the week, as a confirmation that you accept the terms and conditions. Don't do anything stupid. And remember: I know where to find you.

EXT. PRIVATE SCHOOL. DAY

A grand Victorian facade, a wide gravel drive. Tulloch stands on the porch looking at a figure who stands at the gates.

Simon: a copy of the drive in his hand, raised as an ominous warning.

INT. CAR. NIGHT

Simon closes the door.

Tulloch sits, frozen, gazing at the accursed memory stick in his hand.

INT. HOTEL FOYER. NIGHT

Veronika, now dressed with a restrained good taste, waits as Simon approaches.

As he does so, he passes a Concierge, covertly slipping him some cash, fifty pounds or so.

VERONIKA

Well?

SIMON

You are such a dirty hoor.

VERONIKA

That's not nice.

She is entirely unfazed by anything Simon says.

SIMON

Men make easy fools to you, eh?

VERONIKA

I have a lovely idea! You take me out for dinner? Somewhere nice. To make me feel special.

SIMON

And then?

She frowns. Smiles. A tease.

VERONIKA

We'll see.

EXT. EDINBURGH AIRPORT. DAY

A jet lands. Flaps up. Thrusters back. Brakes on.

INT. EDINBURGH AIRPORT. DAY

Travellers step through the arrivals door. There are families waiting for loved ones, and drivers holding names for passengers expected.

A man steps through. Hand luggage only.

He steps beyond the rail and stops, eyes swivelling to make sure there is no one waiting for him.

Mark Renton. Alive. Suit slightly worn but good fit. Shirt and tie.

In front of him are two young Tourism Girls in branded sweatshirts handing out leaflets to anyone who will take them.

They are smiling and enthusiastic.

One of them holds out a leaflet for Renton. He takes it. She speaks with an East European accent.

TOURISM GIRL

Welcome to Edinburgh.

RENTON

Thank you.

The Girl carries on handing out leaflets to other arrivals who pass Renton and her.

He glances through it: a map, a collage of advertising space –
attractions, hotels, B&Bs, wining and dining etc. He folds it up again
and puts it in his pocket.

He watches the Girl handing a leaflet to someone else.

                    RENTON
     Excuse me.

                    TOURISM GIRL
     Yes?

                    RENTON
     Where are you from?

She smiles at him.

                    TOURISM GIRL
     Slovenia.

EXT. EDINBURGH. DAY / INT. TRAM. DAY

Renton watches the city glide into view through the wide windows of
the new tram.

INT. TRAVELODGE CORRIDOR. DAY

Renton turns into the corridor, bag in one hand, plastic key-card in
the other. He finds the door. Dips the key in and opens it.

INT. TRAVELODGE ROOM. DAY

Renton contemplates the small space. Dumps his bag on the bed.

EXT. RENTON FAMILY HOME. DAY

Renton stands in front of the house. Takes it in. Been a long time since
he was here.

INT. RENTON FAMILY HOME. DAY

In the silence, Renton's Father sits opposite his son across the room.

They have not spoken since Renton's arrival.

There are pictures of his parents together, and of him as a child. We may recognise the young boy seen playing earlier.

His father's silent aggression is palpable. There is so much he could say, but in the end he makes simply a bald statement of bitter disappointment.

RENTON'S FATHER
She kept your room, exactly as you left it. She always hoped you'd come back some day.

Renton says nothing. There is nothing to say. Too late for words.

INT. RENTON'S ROOM. DAY

The room is exactly as he left it.

Train wallpaper. Hibs posters. Wardrobe. Record player.

Renton sits on the end of the bed: a middle-aged man transported back to his youth. He is assailed with memories and he just sits, absorbing them all, feeling different and feeling exactly the same all at once.

He kneels down and feels under the edge of the wardrobe – finds what he stashed there a lifetime ago: a quarter of cannabis resin, still in its cling film. He stares at it in his hand.

He notices a pile of football programmes. Picks a couple up. Hibs games from 1988: consecutive weekends. Drops them back down.

Beside that, a neat stack of vinyl albums. His fingers walk through them. Classic and obscure punk, along with the Velvet Underground, Bowie, Lou Reed etc.

He stops at one album, lifts the sleeve and slips out the record. We don't see what it is. He checks the vinyl with that practised but unused glance: no scratches, no warps.

He places the disc on the record player. He switches it on and the disc begins to spin at 33 revolutions per minute. He lifts the little lever and moves the arm across to the edge of the disc. He lowers the stylus and it lands with a damped precision into the outermost groove.

It's turned up loud. Probably always was. The hiss and crackle through the speakers promise imminent violence.

But at the last fraction of a second, or the first promise of the first beat, he flicks up the lever.

He can't listen. Not to that. He hasn't earned it yet.

INT. PRISON CELL. DAY

Begbie lies on his bunk. Waiting. Anger still simmering.

A knock and the voice of Dozo disturbs him.

> DOZO

Franco –

Begbie sits up.

> BEGBIE

C'mon in.

Dozo slips in. Begbie stands up.

> BEGBIE

Are you ready?

> DOZO

Aye, have you got it?

Begbie slips his hand under the mattress and brings out a small sharpened screwdriver.

> BEGBIE

I hope you've no been drinking.

> DOZO

No worries, Franco.

Begbie lifts his shirt and indicates the centre of his abdomen and the right side of his chest.

> BEGBIE

Right. Once here and once here. Not too deep, OK? Just two wee jabs: bit ay blood but no damage, right?

DOZO

Aye, right enough, Franco.

BEGBIE

Do it.

He places the screwdriver in Dozo's hand. Dozo hesitates.

DOZO

You sure?

BEGBIE

Just fucking do it.

Dozo stabs Begbie in the abdomen, but it's too far to the right and it's not a little jab, more like fatal thrust.

Begbie doubles up, clutching his already bloody shirt.

BEGBIE

Aw, ya prick, you've stabbed us in the fucking liver. Oh fucking hell . . .

DOZO

Sorry, Frank! Do you still want me to do the second one?

Begbie is on his knees. Can hardly speak. On the verge of losing consciousness.

BEGBIE

No, Dozo, it's all right, son: I think you've done quite enough already.

EXT. ROAD NEAR SAUGHTON. NIGHT

Ambulance swoops towards the prison. Blue light. Siren.

INT. OPERATING THEATRE. NIGHT

Begbie's abdomen, metal tubes sticking through. Laparoscopic repair in progress.

The Surgeon and Assistant are finding and cauterising the bleeding point.

An Anaesthetist connects up another unit of blood for transfusion.

On the table, asleep and intubated, Begbie looks almost serene.

INT. COUNCIL ESTATE. DAY

A desolate out-of-town estate, a neglected low-rise building.

A Young Man stands outside as Spud approaches.

He gives Spud the nod, and Spud heads on towards a door.

INT. COUNCIL BLOCK STAIRWELL. DAY

The entryphone is long broken and pushing the door brings Spud into a bleak stairwell.

Spud climbs to the first landing.

There are two more Young Men waiting here. Dead-eyed. There is no pretence at social ritual.

One of them extends a hand. Spud places money in it.

The other pulls a small polythene packet from his mouth.

He holds it poised. Spud, desperate, dutifully opens his mouth.

The dealer tucks the polythene packet into Spud's cheek.

The deal is done.

INT. HOTEL ROOM 1. NIGHT

Simon is watching. The props are there. Half-eaten plate of food. Line of cocaine.

On the screen, Veronika is at work.

INT. HOTEL ROOM 2. NIGHT

Veronika and the Punter are undressing, caressing one another. Suddenly the Punter – now naked – notices something.

> PUNTER
> Say, what's that clock for?

VERONIKA

What?

PUNTER

That clock.

VERONIKA

It's nothing – it's just a clock.

PUNTER

Let me see that!

He reaches for it.

INT. HOTEL ROOM I. NIGHT

The picture on the laptop spins around. The audio tells its own story.

VERONIKA
(*out of shot*)

It is nothing. I will put it away –

PUNTER
(*out of shot*)

Hey – what is going on here!

As Simon jumps into action, dashing out of the room.

VERONIKA
(*out of shot*)

Simon!

INT. HOTEL CORRIDOR. NIGHT

Simon exits his room and swipes the lock on the next one.

He rushes in, drawing a small canister of CS gas as he does so.

INT. HOTEL ROOM 2. NIGHT

The Punter, really angry, has one hand around Veronika's throat and the other hand clenched into a fist. It's an ugly scene.

Simon raises the little canister, like a crucifix in an exorcism.

SIMON

Don't fucking touch her!

PUNTER

You in this with her, eh!

He releases Veronika and steps towards Simon. He looks like he could take Simon, if it weren't for the canister, and being naked doesn't help.

Simon holds his chemical weapon out, trembling, as he and the man circle, switching positions until Simon is with Veronika and the man is nearer the door.

Slowly, he picks up his clothes.

PUNTER

See if I hear from you again, you're dead, pal.

Simon, rediscovering some of his initial bravery, steps towards the man, brandishing aggressively.

The man sneers as he walks out the door.

INT. HOTEL CORRIDOR. NIGHT

Carrying his clothes, the Punter walks casually towards the lift.

INT. HOTEL ROOM 2. NIGHT

Veronika has a robe around her. She is sitting on the bed, shaking, sobbing.

VERONIKA

Where were you?

SIMON

Just next door –

VERONIKA

You took a long time.

SIMON

Veronika, I am really sorry. We should get a different camera. That thing looks too obvious.

VERONIKA

I am not doing this again.

SIMON

We'll take a break from it.

VERONIKA

No! Simon – I am not doing this! I feel sick.

SIMON

Veronika: calm down, please. Look – first time, it worked, didn't it?

VERONIKA

I am going back to work for Doyle.

SIMON

Doyle? No, please. You can't do that to me. Not in the sauna.

VERONIKA

Why not?

SIMON

Doyle is a gangster.

VERONIKA

In the sauna, no man would dare to hurt a woman.

SIMON

Veronika, I don't like to think of you working there.

VERONIKA

Why? Because I fuck men? How is this better? I could have been killed! And you would have done nothing because you were sitting next door taking cocaine!

She's righteously furious and Simon has no defence.

VERONIKA

If you love me and respect me, you must help me to do as I wish.

There's not much he can say to that either . . .

VERONIKA
Now, please, I want to go home.

EXT. EDINBURGH. NIGHT

Simon's car – a veteran BMW – rolls into a quiet street and stops.

The door opens. Veronika gets out. She closes the door and heads alone towards a tenement without looking back.

Simon watches her, chastened.

EXT. PORT SUNSHINE. DAWN

The sad pub.

INT. PORT SUNSHINE, BAR. DAY

Simon sits alone behind the bar with a drink.

His gaze rises towards the tobacco-stained ceiling. An idea begins to form in his mind.

INT. PORT SUNSHINE, UPSTAIRS. DAY

Footsteps and a door opens. Ugly strip-lighting flickers on.

Simon looks around the large but dilapidated 'function suite' which currently serves as an oversized glorified store room for broken fruit machines, toilet rolls, cases of cheap wine. Another stair leads up to an attic.

He paces out the size of the huge but useless space.

The idea is growing and growing.

INT. INTENSIVE TREATMENT UNIT. NIGHT

Post-op, Begbie is still connected up to all manner of tubes, drips, drains and monitors.

A G4 Security Officer sits beside the bed, reading a newspaper.

Begbie's eyes open. They dart around, taking in his circumstances. One hand gropes across his abdomen, a tactile inventory of the damage.

His mouth twists into a smile.

EXT. CUL DE SAC. DAY

Renton approaches a small modern house.

INT. GAIL'S HOME. DAY

A comfortable plain living room. A teenage boy – Fergus – sits on the sofa playing a computer game continuously.

Renton sits as Gail, a woman of his own age, passes him a mug of tea before sitting herself.

> RENTON

Thanks.

Gail has let him in, but she's not feeling particularly friendly.

> GAIL

I've no idea.

> RENTON

Right.

An awkward silence. Sip of tea. Bit of biscuit.

> RENTON

Do you think he's using again?

> GAIL

Again? Daniel Murphy? He's never stopped. Paused, sometimes, I'll give him that. But never . . . stopped.

> RENTON

He was a good guy.

> GAIL

The best. When he was around. But mostly he wasn't. Still, that's what it's like, with the heroin.

She looks directly at him.

You'll remember that yourself.

RENTON

Aye.

GAIL

You look all right, Mark.

RENTON

Thanks.

She doesn't mean it as a compliment.

GAIL

See Mark, 'He's done awright tae get out of it.' What Daniel always used to say.

Another pause.

Why do you want to find him?

RENTON

I . . . don't know. Because I'm here, and . . .

GAIL

Old times' sake.

Renton is ashamed.

Gail sighs. Her anger is dissipated.

GAIL

There's a recovery group, meets down by the end of Junction Street. Someone in there might know.

RENTON

Thank you.

GAIL

And if you find him . . . we still love him.

The boy looks up from his game, looking at Renton for the first time.

INT. HOSPITAL ITU. DAY

Begbie is improving, but still connected to his drips and drains.

A big G4 Security Officer sits beside the bed with his newspaper.

A Nurse approaches.

NURSE

Hello, Frank, how are you feeling this morning?

BEGBIE

Bit sore, doll.

NURSE

Well I'm sure we'll soon be able to get rid of some of these tubes.

BEGBIE

Thanks, darling.

He watches her backside as she walks away.

G4 OFFICER

Give us your wrist, Frank: I'm off for a dump.

BEGBIE

Aw, come on, give us a break.

G4 OFFICER

That's the regulations, Frank.

BEGBIE

Where am I going with all these tubes coming out of me? Better than any fucking handcuffs. Give a man a bit of dignity, eh, just for once.

G4 OFFICER

Aye, all right, Frank.

BEGBIE

You're a good man, Officer Lambert, and I respect you for it.

The G4 Officer walks away.

Fucking prick.

He looks around. All the Nurses are busy elsewhere.

First he pulls the drip out of his arm.

Then he yanks the central line from his neck.

And finally he drags the drain from his abdomen.

INT. HOSPITAL CORRIDOR. DAY

Begbie emerges from the Intensive Treatment Unit door.

He is in pain and his gown is bloodstained from the oozing sites but he can walk.

He hobbles along the corridor.

A male Medical Student approaches.

> MEDICAL STUDENT
> Excuse me, sir, are you all right? Can I help?

> BEGBIE
> Aye, you can.

Begbie holds on to the Student to balance himself, then sinks a deep headbutt into him.

INT. HOSPITAL ATRIUM. DAY

In the shiny, spacious PFI atrium, an elevator softly stops.

The doors open. Staff and visitors exit. Last out is Begbie, in the Student's clothes.

A quick glance to left and right. The coast is clear. He presses against the shirt. Blood has oozed through, but no matter.

As he walks towards the exit, he looks the part but the stride is pure thug.

INT. BEDSIT. DAY

Spud is writing a letter. He finishes. Folds it and places it inside a used utility bill envelope, with 'Gail' handwritten on the front.

From a hiding place, he digs out his works. Syringe, needle, spoon, etc.

Stares at them. These are his friends. These are the ones who will never let him down.

INT. DEPARTMENT STORE CAFE. DAY

The smart café of a big store, Jenners or Harvey Nichols.

Veronika sits at a table with Simon. On the seat beside her are the signifiers of a happy shopping trip at Simon's expense, the voluminous, thick paper carriers that hold the designer clothes and shoes.

In between them is laid coffee and an array of expensive pastries. Despite this softening-up exercise, Veronika is less impressed than Simon was hoping.

> SIMON
>
> You will be the manager. The madam.

> VERONIKA
>
> Madam?

> SIMON
>
> It's a word for a woman who is in charge.

> VERONIKA
>
> Madam Veronika. But I don't know, Simon. Is this plan real?

> SIMON
>
> Yes, yes, it is.

> VERONIKA
>
> I believe you are sincere. But perhaps . . . I ought to go home.

> SIMON
>
> I'm going to get builders. Look –

He unfolds a rough drawing. More or less just a rectangle divided by lines.

> SIMON
>
> Partitions. Eight rooms. Sixteen girls. Two shifts. We could be turning over ten thousand pounds a week, every week of the year.

> VERONIKA
>
> So where is my office?

SIMON

What?

VERONIKA

I will need an office. If I am to be *Madam* Veronika –

SIMON

Right. OK . . . that's not a . . .

He takes out a pen and crudely draws another square, ignoring that this is over a previously designed partition.

SIMON

There. Your office is there.

VERONIKA

You have money for all this?

SIMON

Veronika, I will find the money and I will do this for you.

VERONIKA

But when, Simon? I cannot live on a promise.

SIMON

Soon . . . I promise.

She looks at him.

EXT. BEDSIT BLOCK. DAY

Renton looks up at the largely boarded-up, vandalised, dilapidated low-rise block.

This is the depressing place.

INT. BEDSIT BLOCK. DAY

Renton climbs the stairs . . . Finds the right door. It has been previously damaged in a break-in and shoddily repaired.

He knocks. Knocks again. Once more.

No response. Renton is about to give up, but he notices the poor repair and thinks, well, having come this far.

He sticks a key under a piece of ply that has been nailed on and levers it up. The nails ease out and he can just squint through a hole underneath.

INT. SPUD'S BEDSIT. DAY

Renton's point of view: he can see Spud's legs lying outstretched, ankles askew, motionless.

INT. BEDSIT BLOCK. DAY

RENTON

Spud!

It only takes one shove with his shoulder. The Yale bursts open.

INT. SPUD'S BEDSIT. DAY

Spud is lying unconscious on the floor. There is a plastic bag on his head. The syringe and needle lie to one side.

RENTON

Christ!

He tears the bag off and listens to Spud's chest. There might be a heartbeat.

Not knowing exactly what to do . . . he pinches Spud's nose and breathes into his mouth a few times.

He pauses, repeats, now Spud seems to be breathing himself.

Suddenly Spud retches and Renton turns him on his side just in time for the projectile vomit to come out.

Cut to:

INT. SPUD'S BEDSIT. DAY

A little later.

Spud and Renton both seated on the floor, leaning back against the walls.

Renton holds out a damp rag and Spud wipes his face.

SPUD

See what you've gone and done?

RENTON

What?

SPUD

Yeah, you got out all right, didn't you? What about me?

RENTON

I've just saved your life!

SPUD

You ruined my life! And now you've ruined my death.
Thanks, amigo.

RENTON

That is ridiculous! I did what I could for you. Left you four
thousand pounds.

SPUD

Oh, yes, and what did you think I was going to do with it?

RENTON

This is twenty years ago. OK, so you blew it all on drugs.
How can that be my fault?

SPUD

I was a junky, Mark.

Renton stops trying to defend himself.

RENTON

Yeah, I suppose you were.

SPUD

Still am.

*A long silence. Spud wipes his face again. When he speaks again, the
acrimony has vanished.*

SPUD

You look well, though.

RENTON

Everyone says that.

SPUD

Are you staying for a bit?

RENTON

Supposed to be going back in a couple of days' time.

SPUD

Got to stay longer, man! Be good to see you! Spend some time together.

RENTON

I don't know –

SPUD

Missed you, man.

RENTON

Missed you too.

They smile. Spud claps Renton on the shoulder.

RENTON

Don't try and kill yourself again.

SPUD

Not while I got a pal in town. Are you going to see Simon?

Renton affects to have barely considered the matter.

RENTON

Simon? Uh . . . I don't know . . . he's probably busy . . .

SPUD

Naw, you got see old Simon.

RENTON

You know how it is – time goes by –

SPUD

– be gutted not to see you.

RENTON

– He and I, you know how it was, we sorted of drifted apart . . .

SPUD

You and Simon was like that.

Checkmate.

RENTON

Yeah. Like that.

EXT. PORT SUNSHINE. NIGHT

Across the wasteland, Renton watches as the last punter leaves at the end of the evening. The area is deserted.

The pub's outer door is swung shut.

INT. PORT SUNSHINE, BAR. NIGHT

Simon is undertaking what passes for clearing up in here. There is a knock at the door.

He opens it.

Simon stares at Renton. He shows no emotion. Then gestures in.

Renton goes in. The door is closed.

INT. PORT SUNSHINE. NIGHT

Simon and Renton face each other in the empty pub.

SIMON

Well, hello, Mark.

RENTON

Simon.

They sit. It seems cordial, if barbed.

SIMON

So, what you been up to? For twenty years.

RENTON

Oh, where to start? I've been in Amsterdam.

SIMON

Nice.

RENTON

It's all right.

SIMON

What else? Married?

RENTON

Aye.

SIMON

Nice.

RENTON

Dutch woman.

SIMON

Kids?

A fraction of a second of hesitation.

RENTON

Two.

SIMON

Aaaw! Boys or girls?

RENTON

One of each.

SIMON

Lovely. Wee Mark, eh? I'll bet he's a chip off the old block.

RENTON

James, actually. And Laura. How about you?

SIMON

I have a son. He's in London with his fucking hoor mother.

RENTON

See him?

SIMON

Pretty regular. Currently . . . once every ten years.

RENTON

Right.

SIMON

Job?

RENTON

Yeah. I did an accounting course. Work for a small business. Stock management software for the retail sector.

SIMON

Ah. Very nice. Well, as you can see, I'm running my old auntie's pub. Very few customers. They don't spend much. Sometimes it's not even worth opening. The great wave of gentrification has yet to engulf us. But there we go. My lot in life.

RENTON

I see.

Suddenly Simon punches Renton in the face. Renton stumbles back.

SIMON

Ya thieving fucking bastard!

Renton charges.

RENTON

Come on then!

They fight: viciously but amateurishly. It's a pretty even contest. Most punches don't connect but enough of them do.

At one point Simon grabs an empty bottle and breaks it on the edge of the bar.

But he succeeds only in cutting himself.

SIMON

Shit! My fucking hand!

Renton kicks him in the groin. Simon sinks to his knees in agony.

RENTON

You missed a trick, Simon, didn't you? That's what hurts, isn't it – that I had the brains and the balls to steal that money and you didn't!

Simon lurches at Renton's legs. Renton slips.

Simon gets him in a headlock and begins banging Renton's head against the side of the bar.

He shouts to the rhythm of the banging.

SIMON
Six! Teen! Thousand! Pounds! You! Thieving! Fucking! Bastard!

Renton's point of view.

The dark wooden bar looms up again and again.

Smack! Smack! Smack!

Cut to black.

INT. PORT SUNSHINE. NIGHT

Renton's point of view.

His vision is blurred. At first he is aware only of the voice.

VERONIKA
Are you all right?

Her face swims into focus: concerned, intelligent, beautiful. Surely an angel sent from heaven to escort him on his journey.

She fades from view and darkness is restored.

INT. PORT SUNSHINE. NIGHT

Renton opens his eyes.

He sits up, looks around, bewildered. There is no sign of any angel.

Only Simon, sitting at one of the tables, right hand bandaged, chopping out a couple of lines. He snorts the first.

RENTON
Where is she?

SIMON
None of your business. Saved your life, though.

Renton sits down opposite Simon. Watches him.

Simon snorts his second line.

A beat.

Renton reaches into his jacket and lifts out a thickish envelope.

He places it on the table.

> RENTON
> This is for you.

INT. VERONIKA'S FLAT. DAY

A small, neat bedsit.

Simon's rage expressed to Veronika. The cash sits on a table where Simon splayed it out. While Simon rants, Veronika gathers it back into a bundle and places it back in the envelope. She does not appear to be counting it, but she has.

> SIMON
> We did a deal. Back then. Twenty years ago. A couple of bags of H. Good quality stuff. Took it to London. Me, him, Begbie and Spud Murphy. Sold it. Not a bad price. Sixteen thousand pounds. To be divided *in four equal parts*. But he ran off with it, took it all. And now . . . what does he think I am? A whore? Can he pay me off? Four thousand pounds – not even the interest – what am I supposed to do with that? Buy a fucking time machine and live my life all over again, only this time without being betrayed and robbed by my best friend! Doesn't work like that. No . . . what I am going to do, Veronika, is, I am going to draw him back in, as my friend, my very best friend, my partner, and then . . . I am going to hurt him, hurt him in every way I can.

Veronika hands the envelope to Simon.

> VERONIKA
> It's two hundred short.

> SIMON
> I owed someone!

VERONIKA

You bought cocaine.

SIMON

Would you just –

A little sheepish, he tucks the envelope away inside his jacket. Asserts again.

Veronika – I will make him sorry he came back.

INT. SPUD'S BEDSIT. DAY

Renton drops a pair of trainers in front of Spud, who looks at them with suspicion.

EXT. HOLYROOD PARK. DAY

Renton, in his running kit, slightly out of breath, stands on the path around the crags and looks down.

Far below him, Spud is toiling up the steep slope.

EXT. TOP OF ARTHUR'S SEAT. SUNSET

They are seated, watching the yellow glow settle over the city below.

RENTON

You can't just turn up at the door, you know.

SPUD

I know that. She'd no let me in.

RENTON

No, she would let you in – that's the problem. Give you a hot bath and something to eat. Then she'd have to kick you out again after you start stealing from her.

SPUD

I've got to do it right this time. Got to detox the system, man.

RENTON

Detox the system? What does that actually mean? Means nothing. It's not getting it out your body that's difficult. It's getting it out your mind. You're an addict.

SPUD

Mark, I've heard all this. You got twelve steps for me?

RENTON

So be addicted. Be addicted to something else. Anything that's not booze or other drugs.

SPUD

Running until I feel sick?

RENTON

Yes. Or find something better. I'm just trying to help here! You got to channel it, control it. People try all sorts. Like boxing.

SPUD

Boxing?

RENTON

I don't mean that. I mean that's just an example. I don't think you should . . .

SPUD

Boxing.

RENTON

Just something. Anything.

They look out at the city for a beat.

SPUD

So what did you channel it into?

RENTON

Getting away.

SPUD

Nice.

INT. BEGBIE FAMILY HOME, BEDROOM. NIGHT

The bedroom of a flat. A woman sleeps. Middle of the night.

Slowly a window is prised loose and opened. A shadow slips in. He closes the window. The woman wakes, screams!

                              BEGBIE

Shut up, ya cow!

As he switches on the light.

                              JUNE

Frank! Is that you?

                              BEGBIE

Aye, who else is it going to be?

                              JUNE

But the police might be watching!

                              BEGBIE

That's how I come in the back window, woman. Is ma kit still here?

He opens up the wardrobe.

                              JUNE

Of course it is –

                              BEGBIE

Better be.

As he starts emptying the contents of the wardrobe on to the floor, June notices a bloodstain on the student's shirt that Frank is still wearing, reaches forward to touch it.

                              JUNE

Frank –

                              BEGBIE

It's nothing. Get us a plaster or something.

She exits.

At the bottom he finds a large holdall. He opens it up and checks his 'kit' inside.

The bag is stuffed with malicious tools and weapons:

Knives, machetes, cleavers, hammers, pliers, fence-cutters, knuckle dusters, a power drill, plastic ties, gaffer tape, and something about three feet long wrapped in a grey blanket. He peels the blanket back just far enough to confirm the presence of two sawn-off barrels.

June returns with a couple of Elastoplasts.

JUNE

Here – let me –

BEGBIE

Don't fuss me, just get them on –

He settles the kit and zips the bag back up.

The door opens, a gangly twenty-year-old stands there in his underwear, squinting in the light.

FRANK JUNIOR

Dad?

Begbie rises up with a big smile.

BEGBIE

Franco Junior! Let me see ya, ya cuntcha. Ya fucking beauty!

FRANK JUNIOR

But Dad –

BEGBIE

That's right, son, I'm home.

He stands back to admire his work.

FRANK JUNIOR

But what are you going to do?

BEGBIE

Well ah'm no going to sit around all day watchin' the fuckin telly, that's fir sure.

JUNE

But, Frank what if –

BEGBIE

What if what? You and me, Junior, we're going to get out there and do some business.

Mother and son exchange a look.

FRANK JUNIOR

I've . . . enrolled in college, Dad.

BEGBIE

What?

FRANK JUNIOR

Doing a diploma in . . . in Hotel Management.

Begbie looks flummoxed for a beat.

BEGBIE

Ah-ha! Good one. Fuckin' had us there. But seriously, son: you and me, you . . . and me . . . Look at him, June, look at the boy – he cannae fuckin wait!

INT. BEGBIE FAMILY HOME, BEDROOM. NIGHT

Darkness. Begbie and June attempting sex, but it's not working.

Begbie rolls back, exasperated. June whispers, fearful and loving.

JUNE

Never mind, Frank. It's just great to have ye back.

Begbie says nothing.

Abruptly he gets out of the bed and leaves the room.

INT. BEGBIE FAMILY HOME. NIGHT

Now Begbie is sitting in front of the television – no other lights on – a bottle of Beck's in one hand.

He flicks through the channels. Eventually, he settles for one. On the screen is a continuous live roulette show: Supercasino.

He drinks. He watches. He seethes.

Renton, Simon and Veronika are seated at a table for four. Renton's suitcase is to one side.

During Simon's recollections, we may flash to their two seventeen-year-old selves, fleeing, running down Leith Walk.

> SIMON
>
> Do you remember, Mark, that girl, Sharron? Lived in Grantown. Tall. Taller than us, anyway. At the time.

> RENTON
>
> I remember her.

> SIMON
>
> Your very first sexual encounter.

> RENTON
>
> OK.

> SIMON
>
> Mine too.

> RENTON
>
> Right. Is this important?

> SIMON
>
> Do you remember choryin' in Woolworths together? And you got caught and gave my name.

> RENTON
>
> Yeah.

> SIMON
>
> Or that time at Tynecastle we got a kicking off those boys and we thought we were dead? But we fought, didn't we? Sheer desperation. We scrapped our way out of it and ran, and we didn't stop running till we got back to Leith. Fuck, we were scared. And afterwards, just sort of laughing. Couldn't explain it to anyone.

> RENTON
>
> I remember that.

SIMON

Or how about this one? A sunny afternoon. A warm day.
Two young lads. We clubbed together, and we bought our
first hit, off Swanney. Our very first bag of heroin. D'you
remember that?

RENTON

Yes.

SIMON

Swanney's dead now, of course.

RENTON

Be astonished if he wasn't.

SIMON

So we went down that park, back of the banana flats.
Dogshit park.

RENTON

Yeah.

SIMON

We shared a needle.

Renton says nothing. Simon looks him in the eye.

SIMON

We shared a needle . . . and you went first.

Simon snaps with irritation.

Would you stop looking at your watch!

RENTON

I have a flight to catch.

SIMON

Your blood runs in my veins, Mark!

A silent stand-off.

Simon gets up.

Perhaps you'll excuse me for a moment.

INT. GASTROPUB TOILET. DAY

*The inside of a cubicle. Sound of the main door opening and closing,
then the cubicle door opens and Simon enters. He locks the door.*

Simon composes himself after his emotional outburst.

Then he lifts out a bag of cocaine.

INT. GASTROPUB. DAY

Renton and Veronika sip their drinks and look at one another.

> RENTON
>
> So you're Plan B?

> VERONIKA
>
> Yes. I am to persuade you to stay and help him. It will
> mean so much to him to have his oldest friend by his side
> in this exciting new business opportunity.

> RENTON
>
> Did he tell you to say that?

> VERONIKA
>
> Yes.

> RENTON
>
> Did he choose your dress?

> VERONIKA
>
> No. You like it?

> RENTON
>
> It's very nice. Is he taking cocaine in there?

> VERONIKA
>
> Probably.

> RENTON
>
> Is he doing it a lot?

> VERONIKA
>
> As often as he can.

A beat.

46

                              VERONIKA
Simon is not a good person to be in business with.

                              RENTON
No.

                              VERONIKA
But he is your oldest friend. It is difficult for you.

She reaches across the table and squeezes his hand sympathetically.

Renton looks at her.

And he looks over to where Simon went.

Looking back to Veronika again.

INT. GASTROPUB TOILET. DAY

Simon looks in the mirror. Sees that he looks fantastic. A couple of poses. Checks his nostrils. Shoots his cuffs.

INT. GASTROPUB. DAY

The door swings open and Simon strides out.

He stops at the table, dismayed.

                              SIMON
Where is he?

                              VERONIKA
Gone.

                              SIMON
Gone? Gone? How can he be gone? How could you let him go?

He's talking too loud. People are looking round.

                              VERONIKA
Simon.

                              SIMON
How could you let him go! I'm not finished yet! I'm not finished with him!

                                47

He realises that everyone is looking at the shouting man.

What youse fucking staring at! The cunt robbed me of
sixteen thou—

EXT. GASTROPUB. DAY

Simon is ejected from the pub and his coat is thrown after him.

*Veronika, mortified, emerges after him with as much dignity as is
possible.*

She gives him a look that would kill and walks away.

Simon is left talking only to himself.

                    SIMON
    Gone.

INT. AIRPORT CHECK-IN. DAY

Two Tourist Girls handing out promotional leaflets as before.

Far beyond them, at check-in, Renton presents his ticket and passport.

INT. AIRPORT DEPARTURE LOUNGE. DAY

Renton waits to board.

He leafs through the Edinburgh tourist leaflet. He stuffs it into a bin.

                  ANNOUNCER
                  (*on Tannoy*)
    Ladies and gentlemen, Flight EZ042 Edinbugh to
    Amsterdam is now ready for boarding. (*Etc.*)

Renton sits up. He stands, holding his bag. Ready to leave for ever.

He watches the queue form for boarding.

INT. SIMON'S FLAT. DAY

Simon is sitting gloomy and alone, in his underwear, drinking.

Doorbell.

Enter Renton.

SIMON

Mark!

He strides past and turns to face him in the kitchen/living room. The one-and-a-half bedroom flat is an absolute tip. The most disgustingly untidy, food-and-booze-container strewn bachelor pit imaginable. Dirty laundry, sticky floors, nightmare kitchen, crusty bathroom.

Renton is emphatic and impassioned: the first time we've seen the mask of composure slip since he arrived.

As he talks, he is looking around, partly entranced by the mess, but partly looking for something, or someone.

RENTON

I'm getting divorced.

Simon is reeling. Bewildered.

SIMON

You came back to tell me that?

A beat.

Of course, any misfortune that befalls you is music to my ears, but anyway –

RENTON

I was supposed to be going back to move my stuff out. She owns the apartment.

SIMON

What about the children?

A pause.

RENTON

There aren't any.

SIMON

None?

RENTON

No.

SIMON

Oh. So when you said 'Wife, two children, one of each, James and uh . . .'

RENTON

Laura.

SIMON

'Laura' – that wasn't strictly true, was it?

RENTON

No.

SIMON

Why did you lie to me?

RENTON

Because I didn't want to tell you the truth.

SIMON

And the no children thing: was that a problem?

RENTON

None of your business. OK. Yes. Yes. Yes, it was. It was a fucking big problem. All right.

SIMON

These things can tear people apart.

RENTON

Oh fuck off. Tore us apart. That make you happy?

SIMON

Little bit.

RENTON

Anyway, it's over. The marriage. Fifteen years. And the company I work for, that's merged with another. There'll be no room for me. Not enough qualifications. I can see that coming. No need to wait for the fucking letter. So I have nothing, really, and no one, to go back for.

But he's not finished yet.

> And a month ago, I suffered what I've been told was an
> 'episode of acute coronary insufficiency'. Like a heart
> attack. They put a tube in here –

*He pulls down the waist of his trousers just far enough to reveal the
small pink scar.*

RENTON

I have metal stent in my left coronary artery. Good as new,
apparently. Good as new! Should last me another thirty
years, they said. But they never said what I'm supposed to
do with thirty years? Two or three – fine, thanks, I'll take
that, I can cope with that, I can think of enough things to
do to piss away what remains. But thirty? What am I
supposed to do with all that? I'm forty-six, and I am
fucked. I don't have a home. I don't even have anywhere
that I think of as home. I don't really know anyone, don't
really have anyone that I think of as a friend. I look out on
the world and I see strangers. And you . . . you are the . . .
you have the distinction of being – I don't know . . . the
least unfamiliar – that's it.

SIMON

It's better than nothing.

RENTON

And what have you got for me? What is the substance of
our . . . acquaintance –

SIMON

Friendship, please!

RENTON

You invite me to help you with some stupid scheme to
finance, establish and operate a brothel.

SIMON

Sauna. Please.

RENTON

Brothel.

SIMON

Well . . .

RENTON

And the sad thing, the most pathetic aspect of it all, is that
I . . . I can't see anything better. What do I have to look
forward to? What is there? I mean what comes next? More of
the same? Is that it? Oh what joy, what happy fucking days!

SIMON

You're going to help me?

RENTON

Where's Veronika?

SIMON

She's not here.

RENTON

Oh.

SIMON

She doesn't really like staying over. Complains about 'it's a
mess'. That sort of thing.

RENTON

Does she?

SIMON

Not why you stayed, is it?

RENTON

What?

SIMON

Her. Veronika.

RENTON

No. Of course not.

SIMON

Because she's my girlfriend.

RENTON

Right. I know that.

SIMON

Good.

He looks around.

SIMON

It's not a mess, is it?

Renton sees no reason to correct his rival's failings.

RENTON

No. No, it's just . . . masculine.

INT. BOXING GYM. DAY

Spud looks nervous as he stands just inside the entrance, the space not yet revealed.

Now we see where he is. Facing him, eying him up in a V-formation, and not impressed, are half-a-dozen well-toned, hard-as-nails, amateur boxers.

INT. BOXING GYM. DAY

Five minutes later, Spud is in the ring. Big shorts pulled up high. Big gloves on his scrawny limbs.

He raises his guard. He dances a bit from side to side.

The bell rings.

A big gloved fist sails in and hits him right in the face.

EXT. CALTON ROAD. DAY

The door closes behind Spud as he steps out, emotionally and physically stunned.

He is on Calton Road, at the bottom of the hill.

It's not changed much. There's a new office block at the top but it's still a deep canyon running down from Leith Walk with a high arching stone bridge above it.

But the street is deserted. No cars, no people. Silence.

Spud stands for a moment. A memory is creeping over him.

And it has all gone quiet.

He looks down the road in bemusement – then turns abruptly to a shout from above that breaks the silence, where a curving set of steps leads up to the Walk.

Two young men, one then the other, hurtle down the steps, pursued by a man in a store security uniform and a man in a suit.

The first runs right past Spud – oblivious to his presence though close enough for Spud to reach out and touch him – and is nearly hit by a car. The second – it is himself, of course – continues under the bridge, pursued by the suit.

Spud blinks, looks around.

The moment has gone.

EXT. GARDEN. NIGHT

A large stone mansion in one of Edinburgh's desirable leafy enclaves.

Rustling in the undergrowth. Two figures emerge from the bushes and cross the lawn.

Begbie and Frank Junior – wearing masks. Frank Junior carrying the kit bag.

Begbie lifts out a couple of tools and makes quick work of the window latch. Signals to his son – in we go.

INT. LARGE HOUSE. NIGHT

The owner is wealthy.

Begbie and his son have a rucksack each.

Begbie whispers to him.

BEGBIE

Fill the bag – we'll get the telly at the end.

They proceed round the rooms on the lower floor, filling the rucksacks.

Frank Junior knocks over a lamp. Begbie hisses at him.

> BEGBIE

Fir fuck's sake!

> FRANK JUNIOR

Sorry.

> BEGBIE

Shhh!

They stand still for a few moments. Nothing. They carry on, working fast.

Suddenly a voice.

> HOMEOWNER

Hey, what's going on down here?

He's quite a big man, posh, about forty-something. Probably plays rugby. Begbie rushes straight at him.

> BEGBIE

Ya bastard! 'Mon, Junior!

Begbie grabs the guy around the neck and starts laying into him – but Junior just freezes, and the big guy is fighting back. A good punch catches Begbie in the guts.

> BEGBIE

Junior!

But young Frank just stands there, unable to act.

The two men tussle. Begbie will have to settle it himself.

Ach for fuck's sake!

He grabs a heavy ornament and cracks it across the guy's head. A real sickening thud. The Homeowner drops like a stone.

EXT. LARGE HOUSE. NIGHT

Out in the garden, Frank Junior is throwing up. Begbie stands nearby, mask on. Briefly, he checks the puncture wound on his abdomen. Disrupted by the struggle, it oozes slightly.

BEGBIE

You done yet?

FRANK JUNIOR

Think so.

BEGBIE

Right, let's go.

They are setting off.

BEGBIE

Pick up the bag!

FRANK JUNIOR

Sorry.

BEGBIE

Fir fuck's sake.

EXT. LOCKUP. NIGHT

Begbie and Frank Junior stand in the middle of a row of lockups. They have their bulging rucksacks and a large television.

The electric roller door of the lockup in front glides slowly up.

Inside, bathed in light in an Aladdin's Cave of stolen goods, is the malignant squirrel himself, Mikey Forrester.

MIKEY

Franco!

BEGBIE

Mikey!

The two bams greet each other with hugs and mock punches. There is a lot of 'yacuntchas'.

Begbie calls to his son.

BEGBIE

Hey, bring the telly in.

Junior lurches in with the big television.

MIKEY

Who's this, then?

Begbie puts an arm around his son.

BEGBIE

This big handsome bastard is none other than my son.
Frank Junior, meet Mikey Forrester!

MIKEY

Teaching him the trade then, Frank?

BEGBIE

Aye, well he's got a bit of catching up to do.

MIKEY

You're in good hands there, son.

BEGBIE

He's got the talent, all right. We had a bit of bother.
Concerned citizen came downstairs, tooled up 'n aw. I was
on the back foot, I can tell you, but Frank Junior here took
him out and no mistake.

MIKEY

Is that right? Well done, son –

FRANK JUNIOR

Well, it wisnae quite –

Begbie slaps him on the back.

BEGBIE

Takes after his old man!

EXT. LOCKUP. NIGHT

*Begbie and Junior are walking away. Begbie stuffing a wad of cash
into his jacket. He stops.*

BEGBIE

I covered up for you there.

FRANK JUNIOR

Sorry, Dad.

See if that happens again, son or no son, be fuckin' kicking. Right?

Yes, Dad.

Right. Come on.

INT. BEGBIE FAMILY HOME, BEDROOM. NIGHT

In darkness, a man on top of a woman. But he rolls off with a sigh and a curse.

JUNE

Never mind, Frank.

BEGBIE

Aw, fuckin' shut up.

JUNE

It's no' your fault.

BEGBIE

Course it's no' ma bloody fault. No one says it was ma fault.

He sits on the side of the bed.

Are you sayin' it's ma fault?

JUNE

No, Frank! No! Honestly.

BEGBIE

Just as well.

JUNE

You kin get, you know, pills fir it.

BEGBIE

Pills! Pills! What am ah wantin' fuckin' pills for? Ahm no some fuckin' junky. Pills.

INT. BEGBIE FAMILY HOME. NIGHT

Begbie. Beck's. Television: Supercasino.

EXT. CUL DE SAC. DAY

Spud approaches Gail's house.

He rings the doorbell and waits.

Gail answers it. She was expecting him. Her emotions are mixed.

> GAIL

Hello.

> SPUD

Hi.

His shame is too much for her.

> GAIL

Do you want to come in?

Spud is about to – but checks himself.

> SPUD

Eh – no, actually. Probably better I . . . I'm trying to . . . you know.

She nods. Yes, she knows.

> SPUD

Did you manage to –

> GAIL

Aye, I found it for you.

She disappears for a few seconds and returns with a plastic bag containing something, like envelopes packed together.

> SPUD

Aw, that's great. I hope it didn't . . . you know.

> GAIL

It was no trouble.

Another pause. There isn't much that hasn't been said before.

SPUD

Maybe another time, I'll –

He gestures, meaning 'go inside'.

GAIL

I'd like that.

SPUD

Send my love to Fergus.

GAIL

He's not in, otherwise I would have –

SPUD

No, it's all right – I wouldn't have wanted to disturb anyone.

GAIL

Take care, Daniel.

SPUD

Aye, you too.

She closes the door.

INT. SPUD'S BEDSIT. NIGHT

Spud lifts the assorted old envelopes, three or four of them at most, from the plastic bag.

He delves into one of the envelopes at random – and lifts out a photograph.

It is an old image, not a great quality shot, slightly blurred, red eye, but there they are, Spud and Tommy, or Spud and Renton, on some joyous bender together, more than twenty years earlier.

The envelopes are all filled with old photographs, and with scraps of paper – torn from a wide variety of notebooks, Post-its, wrapping paper, etc. – on which, at one time or another in the past, Spud has written phrases, words, names, even the odd sentence or two, the origins of which will become clear.

EXT. LOYALIST CLUB. NIGHT

*A car – Simon's old BMW – is parked across the road from an
unremarkable pub/social club.*

INT. SIMON'S CAR. NIGHT

*Veronika is in the driver's seat. In the back, Simon is carefully
inscribing something on Renton's arm with a dark blue marker pen.*

>   RENTON
> It's a fixed point, you see, a certainty. These are people who
> have been abandoned by their political class, but at least
> they have what we don't – a sense of identity.

>   SIMON
> Come on, Mark. Let's get it over with.

>   RENTON
> An identity encapsulated in four digits.

He shows Veronika his arm: 1690.

*Simon – who has a similar 'tattoo' – removes the small crucifix from
around his neck and hands it to Veronika.*

They both hand over their phones.

>   RENTON
> It's all on there for you.

>   SIMON
> If we're not out in one hour, call the police.

>   VERONIKA
> What shall I say?

>   SIMON
> Just tell them we're dead.

*They get out. She watches them cross towards the pub. She looks at
Renton's phone in her hands. She taps a couple of choices. A video.*

Renton's face appears on the screen of the phone.

INT. SOCIAL CLUB. NIGHT

Renton and Simon take it all in.

A local Orange Lodge social night.

1690 is everywhere: on flags, tattoos, knuckles, the drums, etc. A large flag has King William superimposed over the Union Jack.

There's a band playing, a mixture of popular covers, American country, and Loyalist anthems.

INT. SIMON'S CAR. NIGHT

Veronika watches Renton on the screen of his phone. He recorded the video (on his phone, just before they went out) in Simon's flat. Simon – oblivious – may occasionally appear deep in the background, searching for his socks or something.

> RENTON
> The Battle of the Boyne was fought on 11th July 1690 between two rival claimants of the British and Irish thrones – James II . . . and William of Orange –

INT. SOCIAL CLUB. NIGHT

Renton and Simon buy drinks at the bar. They merge with the crowd. They join in the singing with gusto. They are to all appearances devout Orangemen.

But they are also stealing.

When men get up to sing/dance, one shields the other who dips a hand through a jacket or coat. A wallet or purse is quickly filleted – cards removed – and replaced.

Each time they do this carries the possibility of being caught and battered senseless.

INT. SIMON'S CAR. NIGHT

Veronika watches as the lecture continues.

RENTON

The battle is seen as the decisive end to James II's attempt
to regain the crown and ultimately ensured the continuation
of the Protestant supremacy in Ireland . . .

INT. SOCIAL CLUB. NIGHT

The thieving and the singing continue.

INT. SIMON'S CAR. NIGHT

RENTON

Yet victory has perhaps cost the winners as much as the
losers, for an uncompromising commitment to a sense of
Protestant destiny has left them estranged from the modern,
secular, progressive United Kingdom.

INT. SOCIAL CLUB. NIGHT

Simon and Renton share a look – that's enough.

*They make their way casually towards the exit – but find their way
barred by a Big Bear and his friendly paw.*

BIG BEAR

Going to give us song, lads?

INT. SIMON'S CAR. NIGHT

RENTON

But if nothing else, history has shown us very clearly –
these are people whom it is unwise to provoke.

INT. SOCIAL CLUB. NIGHT

Renton and Simon on stage. You can hear a pin drop.

*Simon picks up an acoustic guitar as if full of purpose. To fill the
silence he strums a random chord.*

*Renton at the microphone. He looks out on a small sea of expectant
faces. Faces not to be disappointed. Or provoked.*

As Simon strums again, Renton improvises a line. Badly.

RENTON

'Twas in the year of 1690 . . . upon the 11th of July . . . or
1st in the Julian calendar . . . '

Simon glares at him: for fuck's sake, Mark . . .

*Lyrically, there's no turning back here. Renton gropes his way forward,
hoping for inspiration.*

Upon the field of battle, of hope we were bereft . . .

Suddenly he sees a way out of this cul-de-sac.

But by the time that it was over . . . THERE WERE NO
MORE CATHOLICS LEFT!

A huge cheer – they love it!

INT. SIMON'S CAR. NIGHT

Renton continues on the screen of the phone.

RENTON

As a political force they have supported the Union – only to
find that the Union no longer really cares for their support.

INT. SOCIAL CLUB. NIGHT

*Renton continues, gaining in confidence, strolling across the stage,
shoehorning each couplet towards its popular finish.*

RENTON

They gazed up to King William, upon his chin a royal cleft /
And by the time that it was over, there were no more
Catholics left!

And more, if necessary.

His leadership was brave, his strategy was deft, / And by the
time that it was over, there were no more Catholics left!

INT. SIMON'S CAR. NIGHT

Renton reaches his conclusion.

> RENTON
> And faced with an uncertain future, is it any surprise that
> they find comfort in the past, searching for relevance in the
> twenty-first century while looking back to the seventeenth?

INT. SOCIAL CLUB. NIGHT

*The place is rocking now. Sweat-drenched showman Renton has the
audience in the palm of his hand now – conducting them in a
singalong, with different groups, men/women/young/old, singing in the
round, harmonising etc.*

*Meanwhile Simon has swapped acoustic for electric and is shredding
wildly.*

> RENTON / CROWD
> No more Catholics / No more Catholics / No more
> Catholics . . . No more! / No more! / No more / No more! /
> No . . . more . . . Catholics . . . leeeeeeeeft!

Massive applause.

EXT. WASTELAND AND PUB. NIGHT

Simon and Renton sprinting as fast as they can towards the car.

INT. SIMON'S CAR. NIGHT

They pull the doors shut.

> SIMON
> Just fucking drive.

EXT. BANK. NIGHT

*A silent, deserted high street in the middle of the night. Veronika's car
parked nearby.*

At the ATM. Cards going in one after the other . . . Fingers typing into the keypad:

. . . 1690 . . . 1690 . . . 1690 . . . 1690 . . .

Wads of £250 a time coming out . . . over and over again. The few cards for which 1690 does not work are discarded without a second glance.

Renton checks his watch.

> RENTON
>
> And . . . midnight.

They start to raid the cards all over again . . .

EXT. MOTORWAY. NIGHT

Veronika's car speeds along the motorway towards Edinburgh.

Simon and Renton are giving it the full pantomime.

> RENTON
> (*out of shot*)
> So this room service guy comes in, and there's George
> Best, lying in bed –

INT. SIMON'S CAR. NIGHT

Simon is flicking a bundle of notes right up close to his eye.

Renton, sitting in the back with him, is trying to explain to Veronika.

> RENTON
> – with two *Playboy* models, drinking champagne.

> SIMON
> I love this story.

> RENTON
> Three in a bed, champagne, bit of Charlie, and there's
> banknotes. They're lying on them.

> VERONIKA
> Lying on the money?

RENTON

Yes.

VERONIKA

Why?

RENTON

I don't know. Because he has lots of money. Or at least he did. At the time.

VERONIKA

It seems foolish.

RENTON

It's what they're doing. Three in a bed. Sex. Drugs. Alcohol. Money.

VERONIKA

And that is the story?

RENTON

No! No, no, that's just the background. The room service guy comes in, and he looks at the scene – which I have just described – and he says: 'George Best –'

SIMON

'– greatest footballer of all time –'

RENTON

Yes '– greatest footballer of all time – I have to ask you . . . where did it all go wrong?'

He and Simon crack up, repeating the punchline. They do love that story.

Eventually:

VERONIKA

But I think that the room service guy . . . he makes a very good point.

EXT. VARIOUS FOOTBALL PITCHES. DAY

A medley of wonderful George Best goals and moments, with fruity old style commentators.

Ooh, that is simply wonderful from Best . . . (*etc.*)

INT. SIMON'S FLAT. NIGHT

Simon, Renton, and a slightly less fascinated Veronika are watching YouTube on Simon's laptop.

Exhilarated by their success, they are making a night of it. They have:

George Best on YouTube.

Their favourite music from the past booming loud.

Cocaine.

Vodka.

The cash proceeds are stacked on a table for all to see.

Renton explains.

RENTON

He played for Hibs. 1979. In between stints for the Fort Lauderdale Strikers and the San Jose Earthquakes. I saw him play. Apparently. My dad took me. 'You got to see this. Got to see this player. The greatest footballer of all time.' Big crowd, big guy in front of me, I couldn't see a thing. Not a single thing. Not for ninety minutes. Got the programme though. Always got that . . .

And later. Off their heads, they talk nonsense with neither listening to the other.

RENTON

Look . . . thin . . . thin . . . thin . . . thin . . . no one was fat in those days . . . there was no such thing as calories until about 1974, you know what happened in 1974, the first-ever McDonald's opened in the UK. Look: thin . . . thin . . .

SIMON

What he's about, I mean it's not just the football, is it? It's the end of austerity, the end of rationing, welcome to the new world of civil rights and space exploration. Basically he's John Barry with football boots. I mean you listen to that tune, it's a

thin. That guy – nowadays that would be scrawny but that was normal till 1974, you know what happened then. First McDonald's. South London. Woolwich. It's still there. I've been to it several times.

great swaggering filthy piece of music. It's insurrection, and that's what he is too. That is the beauty of what he does. He is the herald of a new age. These are not goals, these are political statements.

Etc.

And Veronika, with rapid fire sub-titles:

VERONIKA
(in her own language)
You know nothing. You understand nothing. You are quite clearly so in love with one another that I feel almost awkward even in your presence. Why do you pretend to hate each other so much when all you want is to be together? Instead of looking at me why don't you just take your clothes off and get on with it.

The men understand not a word. And later, she adds:

VERONIKA
(in her own language)
You live in the past. Everyone here lives in the past. Where I come from the past is something to forget but here it's all you talk about. That and the weather. So boring.

Now they are re-enacting George Best's goals with the sofa as the goal.

Now they are dancing, air guitar to their favourite song.

Now they are ransacking a cupboard in search of something.

Now they find it – the old air rifle.

Now Simon has the air rifle and is firing it into a cushion that Renton holds in front of his face, laughing and flinching with the impact.

Now it's Renton's turn to fire the air rifle at Simon.

Now Veronika's turn while both men hold up cushions and her aim swings from one to the other.

Their favourite music continues loud over everything.

More George Best, more cocaine, more vodka, more re-enactments, more of everything.

Now Simon is out cold and Renton is watching the computer with a memory drive stuck into the side.

He is watching (on the computer screen) Veronika (although her face is not visible) and Tulloch. He looks up, to see Veronika looking at him, realises it is her on the screen.

Now Simon and Renton have their arms draped around each other's necks, singing into each other's faces.

And Veronika has gone.

Now Simon awakes from his stupor, sits bolt upright and says.

SIMON
That is not a goal, that is a political statement.

EXT. FOOTBALL STADIUM. DAY

Silence.

A final George Best goal fills the screen, all its perfection in silent slow motion.

INT. SPUD'S BEDSIT. NIGHT

Spud pins a photograph to the wall. He sits back, on the floor, and looks up at the wall in front of him.

It is covered in a mosaic of the old photographs: himself, Renton, Simon, Begbie, Tommy, Gail, Gav, Swanney, all captured and immortalised.

And in front of him, arranged like a jigsaw, the assembled notes, words and memos, the collected works of Spud Murphy.

INT. BEGBIE FAMILY HOME. NIGHT

Begbie is standing by the door with his kit bag ready to go out, irritated by being kept waiting.

Junior! Junior! Fir fuck's sake . . . are you coming?

June appears from the living room doorway.

JUNE

Frank –

BEGBIE

What? What is it now?

JUNE

The boy . . .

BEGBIE

What about him. Junior!

JUNE

See Frank, please, don't be angry, it's just he's no . . .

BEGBIE

No what?

Frank Junior appears. He and June are intensely nervous.

FRANK JUNIOR

Sorry, Dad.

BEGBIE

What is this? What's going on? You're no going out in those clothes.

FRANK JUNIOR

I'm no' sure if I'm really, you know, into it.

JUNE

He disnae want to go, Frank.

Begbie does not understand.

BEGBIE

So what are you going to do instead?

FRANK JUNIOR

Just thought I might, you know, meet some friends from the college.

BEGBIE

Fae the college? Right. Well that's a blow and no mistake.
I can tell you.

FRANK JUNIOR

I'm sorry, Dad.

BEGBIE

Some way to treat your old man.

JUNE

Please, Frank –

BEGBIE

YOU SHUT UP! Hotel Fucking Management. You put
him up to this.

FRANK JUNIOR

Dad – it's no' like that –

BEGBIE

Shut up. 'Dad'! Maybe I'm no' your dad. I see it now.

JUNE

No, Frank!

FRANK JUNIOR

Leave it, Dad!

BEGBIE

Leave it? *Leave it?* Oh . . . So what if I don't want tae leave
it, what are you gaunnae do? OK . . . Free pop. Come on:
stick one on us then, ya cunt.

*He waits, arms open, ready to be hit, but Frank Junior does not do it.
Begbie sneers.*

BEGBIE

You huvnae got it, huv ye. If you were ma son, you'd have
chibbed us there. I'd be lying there breathing out my last
through a hole in my chest. But you cannae do that. Hotel
Management. I gave you the wrong name, pal, because as
every cunt knows, there's only one Frank Begbie.

72

EXT. SIMON'S FLAT. DAY

A police car pulls up outside the Leith tenement.

Two Police Officers get out.

We follow them into the tenement . . .

INT. SIMON'S FLAT, LANDING. DAY

. . . and up the stairs to the second or third floor to reach the door of Simon's flat.

One of them presses the buzzer.

Simon opens the door. He is wearing his underwear.

He looks at the two Police Officers.

> SIMON
>
> What do you want?

INT. TRAVELODGE CORRIDOR. DAY

A Cleaner hoovering.

INT. RENTON'S HOTEL ROOM. DAY

Renton lies in the plain small room, listening to the Hoover, regretting the excesses.

His phone rings.

> RENTON
>
> Hello . . . What? When? Aw, no.

INT. POLICE STATION. DAY

Simon on the phone.

> SIMON
>
> Mark – I need a lawyer.

INT. SOLICITOR'S OFFICE. DAY

Renton and Veronika sit patiently. Renton is a little uncomfortable for reasons that will become clear.

The office is neat but there are stacks of files everywhere.

On the desk, a woman's hand holds the couple of pages on which the charges are listed. And now we see her face.

> DIANE
>
> So. As I understand it, the complainant, who is the deputy headmaster at a private school here in Edinburgh, alleges that he has been the victim of attempted extortion. How does Sick Boy intend to plead?

> RENTON
>
> It's Simon now.

> DIANE
>
> Right. Simon.

> RENTON
>
> Not guilty.

> DIANE
>
> Fine. Off the record, the police have told me that the USB drive does have Simon's prints on it and that in searching the flat they found the mobile that the bank details were sent from.

> RENTON
>
> I see.

> DIANE
>
> As well as the cocaine, of course.

> RENTON
>
> That was only personal use.

> DIANE
>
> Quite a lot for personal use.

> RENTON
>
> Well, you know Simon.

DIANE

I certainly remember him. Does he still take heroin?

RENTON

No.

DIANE

Do you?

RENTON

No. Not for twenty years.

DIANE

That's really good. I'm glad you've managed to turn your life around.

She turns her attention to Veronika.

DIANE

So are you the woman in the video?

VERONIKA

My face is not seen.

DIANE

You are visible only from behind?

VERONIKA

Yes.

DIANE

Do you have any identifying marks? Tattoos on your buttocks?

VERONIKA

Certainly not.

DIANE

On your perineum?

VERONIKA

Sorry?

Renton leans over and whispers in her ear.

That is disgusting.

DIANE

It's fashionable. Amongst a certain type.

VERONIKA

I would not know that type.

DIANE

So you're not vajazzled?

Veronika just meets that with a glare.

Well, perhaps the woman in the video will never be
identified and never called upon to give evidence, unless
the judge asks to see you au naturel. May I ask, what is
your relationship with the accused?

VERONIKA

We are friends.

DIANE

Right.

*Diane takes a long look at Veronika. She makes a note, then swivels
and looks Renton in the eyes.*

DIANE

Mark?

RENTON

Nothing to add.

DIANE

Well, I think a defence can be constructed here, but it's not
straightforward. With regard to the blackmail, perhaps
Simon will tell us that the recording was consensual, and
was in fact commissioned by the complainant, hence the
request for payment. We might pursue that line, in return
for which, Simon might plead guilty on the cocaine. The
amount is way over for personal and they will press for
intent to supply, and go after the proceeds but, remarkably,
this is a first offence and there are no other aggravating
factors. If Simon cooperates and enters into an approved
rehabilitation scheme, he might escape with a thousand-
pound fine and a suspended sentence.

RENTON

That would be –

DIANE

This consultation is free. Should we go forward, my own
fees are two hundred and fifty pounds an hour plus VAT.
Where possible, I will delegate to our paralegal secretary
whose work is charged at eighty pounds per hour. I will also
have to instruct an advocate, of course, to actually
represent Simon in court –

RENTON

Sorry – how much is –

DIANE

About the same.

RENTON

Right.

DIANE

Shall we proceed?

INT. SOLICITOR'S OFFICE RECEPTION. DAY

On the way out.

DIANE

Mark.

Renton, summoned, returns, obedient but weary.

RENTON

Yes.

Diane whispers in his ear.

DIANE

She's too young for you.

INT. LAWYER'S HOUSE. DAY

A middle-class home.

Begbie's lawyer, Stoddart – still wearing a neck brace after the assault – is busy getting ready to leave his flat.

He gathers up his bag, coat etc. and heads for the door.

He opens the door – and finds himself shoved back.

Begbie walks in. Drops his bag. Closes the door behind him.

> STODDART
>
> Frank!

> BEGBIE
>
> Mr Stoddart. Quite a place you got here, all by yourself an' all. Legal aid, eh? Nice work if you can get it.

> STODDART
>
> Frank – we need to call the police right now and agree a return to Saughton.

> BEGBIE
>
> I'm no' doin' that.

> STODDART
>
> Your presence here puts me in a difficult position.

Begbie steps towards the terrified man.

> BEGBIE
>
> Difficult position? Aye. Right enough.

INT. SPUD'S BEDSIT. DAY

Spud sits against the wall, opposite his collage.

He has a torn-out sheet of lined paper on the floor between his legs and a pencil in his hand.

He leans forward awkwardly and writes.

'Kicking –'

He underlines it and then below:

'The sweat was lashin offay Sick Boy . . .'

He scribbles away, his hand struggling to keep up with his thoughts.

INT. SIMON'S FLAT. DAY

Simon, in his underwear as usual, watches Renton who is sitting at the table with a laptop.

RENTON

Here it is: 'EU Small Business Development Loan. Zero-interest loans distributed regionally, towards projects that stimulate regeneration of formerly industrial areas. Loans are available of up to fifty thousand pounds. Application should be made online, which may be followed by an invitation to present a business plan . . .'

SIMON

Blah blah fucking blah.

RENTON

I'm trying to help, Simon.

SIMON

You could have got someone cheaper.

RENTON

Yes, and if you hadn't engaged in blackmail, I wouldn't have had to get anyone at all. The ten thousand is basically gone. What about the four thousand?

SIMON

I have expenses like anyone else.

RENTON

All of it? You've snorted the whole fucking wad?

SIMON

The point is that we need cash. Now! Not in six months' time! Do you not realise what is at stake here? I have promised to set up a sauna for Veronika and if I don't get it up and running – soon – she is going to leave me.

RENTON

She's going to leave you anyway.

SIMON

No . . . No . . . That is not going to happen.

RENTON

Is she actually with you?

SIMON

She's my girlfriend.

RENTON

You've never even knobbed her.

SIMON

I have knobbed her and I will knob her again.

RENTON

What, when she was working at the sauna?

SIMON

That is unfair. Actually, since we're having this conversation, I can tell you that fully consensual, emotionally driven, not-for-profit sexual intercourse has been attained.

RENTON

God, you're romantic.

SIMON

Veronika and I have had our rough patches, I'd be the first to admit that.

RENTON

Shall we submit this application?

SIMON

Do what you want but I need someone, on-site, working . . . I need progress!

EXT. PORT SUNSHINE. DAY

Morning. Still closed. Spud knocks on the door.

Renton opens it from inside, smiling at the expected visitor.

RENTON

Come on in, Spud.

INT. PORT SUNSHINE, UPSTAIRS. DAY

Simon is near the door, muttering to himself.

> SIMON
> This . . . this . . . this feckless, useless, incompetent,
> unreliable, untrustworthy, wasted, fucked-up, junky –

> VERONIKA
> Simon? You have something to say?

> SIMON
> No. Nothing.

He takes his cue. The door closes.

> VERONIKA
> When clients come in, I want a sense of space.

> SPUD
> And soft light. To make them feel relaxed.

> VERONIKA
> Exactly. I am so glad that someone understands.

INT. LAWYER'S HOME, AIRING CUPBOARD. NIGHT

Stoddart, bruised and terrified, is in that difficult position, tied to the pipes with plastic ties.

Begbie stands over him, reading from a thick legal textbook.

> BEGBIE
> 'An aberration or weakness of the mind, bordering on
> though not amounting to, insanity . . . a mind so affected
> that *responsibility is diminished*. In other words, the prisoner
> is only partially accountable for his actions.' See, if I can
> say it, how could you no'?

And he raises the heavy book as if to strike Stoddart again.

Stoddart whimpers, sobs, attempts to shield his head with his one free hand.

Begbie draws it out, the anticipation, then sneers.

He throws the textbook to the floor. Stoddart jolts as if hit himself.

The door closes. Stoddart opens his eyes. This nightmare will never end.

INT. LAWYER'S HOUSE. NIGHT

Begbie opens a beer and takes his place on the big seat opposite the television.

He flicks it on: Supercasino.

INT. PORT SUNSHINE, UPSTAIRS. DAY

Spud bringing in timber, plasterboard, reels of cable, copper pipes, tools etc.

INT. DEPARTMENT STORE CAFÉ. DAY

Renton and Veronika sitting by a window in the bright, busy café of Jenners or Harvey Nichols.

She has a shopping bag, an expensive thick paper one from a designer concession. Inside is a handbag.

Between them: coffee and the expensive pastries.

> VERONIKA

Thank you.

> RENTON

It's nothing.

She briefly puts a hand on his across the table. That innocent gesture again.

> VERONIKA

No, really, you have been very kind. This one, I will keep.

She serves pastries on to two plates.

What did that lawyer say to you?

> RENTON

That I am too old for you.

And are you?

RENTON

You tell me.

VERONIKA

Shall I be honest?

RENTON

Let's drink our coffee.

They drink.

VERONIKA

Simon and I do not sleep together.

RENTON

I wondered.

VERONIKA

Once. But . . .

She makes a face, neither good nor bad.

RENTON

So now?

VERONIKA

I am his girlfriend. But it is business, really. He is not a
good person.

RENTON

No. Not at all.

VERONIKA

But I like him. More than he likes himself, I think.

RENTON

Right. But if you're not, I mean if there is no physical
dimension to the relationship, are you not – I mean it's not
for me to say, but you don't want to be wasting your time –

VERONIKA

What is 'choose life'?

What?

'Choose life.' Simon says it sometimes. He says it to me:

She imitates Simon imitating Sean Connery.

'Choosh life, Veronika . . .'

Ah. Yes. 'Choose life'. It was . . . it was the well-meaning slogan from a 1980s anti-drugs campaign that we, as heroin addicts, appropriated in a way that we thought was ironic and we used to add things to it, to underscore our belief that the notion of choice was being falsely represented . . . so I might say, for example –

He looks around, takes inspiration at first from the bags on the chair beside her, then more generally as he becomes more impassioned.

Choose designer lingerie in the vain hope of kicking some life back into a dead relationship. Choose handbags, high-heeled shoes, cashmere and silk to make yourself feel what passes for happy, choose an iPhone made in China by a woman who jumped out a window, and stick it in the pocket of your jacket fresh from a South Asian firetrap, choose Facebook, Twitter, Snapchat, Instagram and a thousand other ways to spew your bile across people you've never met, choose updating your profile, tell the world what you had for breakfast and hope that someone somewhere cares, choose looking up old flames, desperate to believe that you don't look as bad as they do, choose liveblogging from your first wank to your last breath, human interaction reduced to nothing more than data, choose recording everything, remembering nothing, and plugging yourself into reality TV because their struggles have become your own. Choose ten things you never knew about celebrities who've had surgery, choose screaming about abortion, choose rape jokes, slut-shaming, revenge porn, and an endless tide of depressing misogyny, choose 9/11 never happened and if it did it was the Jews. Choose standing at the gates of the rich staring in at the Lamborghinis. Choose a zero-hours contract and a two-hour journey to work. Choose the same for your kids, only worse, and maybe tell yourself it's better they never happened. Then take a deep breath in and smother all the pain with an unknown dose of an unknown drug made in someone's kitchen. Maybe that'll help. Or maybe it won't, but then nothing else will either. Choose unfulfilled promise and wishing you'd done it all differently, choose failing to learn from your own mistakes, choose watching history repeat itself, choose the slow reconciliation towards what you can get rather than what you always hoped for. Settle for less and keep a brave face on it. Choose disappointment. Choose losing the ones you loved, and as they fall from view, a piece of you dies with them, until you can see that in the future, one day, piece by piece they will all be gone and there will be nothing left of you to call alive or dead.

He checks himself.

Anyway, it kept us amused at the time.

Veronika is gazing blankly out of the window.

He shuts up.

Eventually she returns her gaze to him and smiles.

                              VERONIKA
I like you, Mark.

INT. PORT SUNSHINE, UPSTAIRS. DAY

Spud is preparing to work.

But first he must clear the rubbish out from one end.

He lifts aside some boxes. There is a shape covered by a sheet. He pulls it and reveals underneath an old jukebox.

He plugs it in. It lights up. Clicks and whirrs into life. He finds a coin left in the refund slot.

He feeds it in.

It plays an old soulful classic.

And Spud begins to sing . . .

His voice soars with emotion, takes over from the jukebox.

Intercut with:

Deliveries of supplies of timber, plasterboard, copper pipe, electrical cable, tools etc.

Simon handing over cash to delivery guys.

Spud's associates from the recovery group arriving to help with construction.

Simon handing over cash to the recovery guys.

Spud and co. working – the timber skeleton taking shape, the plasterboard panels being fixed into place.

Begbie and Stoddart: Begbie feeding his prisoner/host.

Simon and Renton: on the sofa watching a DVD.

Veronika inspecting the progress.

Spud, alone, singing.

And then, Gail is there, as Spud sings. But as he finishes the song, she has gone.

INT. PORT SUNSHINE, UPSTAIRS. DAY

Spud resumes work, drills home a screw with power tool.

He stands back and we can see – it's nearly done.

INT. VERONIKA'S APARTMENT. DAY

Renton and Veronika are lying in bed together.

> RENTON
> It's true. I stole the money. Shouldn't have been a surprise.
> We stole from lots of people: shops, businesses, neighbours,
> family. 'Friends' was just one more class of victim.

A beat.

What are you going to do?

VERONIKA

I am to be the madam in Simon's bordello.

RENTON

But really.

VERONIKA

I should go home. But to go home, with nothing, no qualification, no career, not even bringing money . . .

RENTON

What's at home?

VERONIKA

Oh, you know: emotional attachment.

RENTON

Right.

VERONIKA

That's all.

INT. LAWYER'S HOME. DAY

Close up: a knife on a carpet.

Stoddart's hand slams down on the carpet as, just out of shot, he grunts with the effort, but the fingers fall just millimetres tantalisingly short. The hand withdraws, tries again. And fails.

Stoddart is attached to the heating pipe with a cable tie around one wrist. With an exhausting lurch, he can almost reach the object of salvation. But not quite.

He keeps on trying. Maybe he will get there in the end.

INT. PORT SUNSHINE. DAY

Simon resentfully serves a pint to one of the handful of ageing clientele.

As he turns to fill a whisky from the rack, he sees a figure in the mirror. Sort of familiar at first . . . cap and shades but . . .

He turns with a face full of dread. He can barely get the words out.

SIMON

Hello . . . Franco.

BEGBIE

Simon.

Oh no. Oh fucking no . . .

SIMON

But you're not . . .

BEGBIE

I'm out.

SIMON

Out?

BEGBIE

Aye – Shhhh . . .

INT. PORT SUNSHINE, OFFICE. CELLAR

Simon shuts the trap. He turns to the man he followed down here, where the barrels are stored.

The vital few seconds have given him time to think as he chops out a couple of lines for himself and Begbie.

Begbie takes off the shades and hat. While they converse, they snort the coke.

SIMON

Sorry if I seemed a little shocked to see you, Franco, it's just that . . .

A thought forms in his mind.

Well . . . I was going to deal with this myself and then let you know the good news but . . . you won't believe this, two days ago, I got a call from an old friend – Gav Temperly, remember him?

BEGBIE

Aye.

SIMON

Well – he was on business, in Amsterdam. He was in a café one morning, and he heard this voice beside him.

BEGBIE

Right –

SIMON

A whiney, cunty voice –

BEGBIE

No!

SIMON

Aye. So he turns around – this is two days ago – I'm still getting over it myself – And there he is. *There he is.*

BEGBIE

Holy fucking moly.

SIMON

Hasn't changed in twenty years. Same smug little cunty grin across his ugly face –

BEGBIE

Fir fuck's sake!

SIMON

Renton. Mark fucking Renton. Living in Amsterdam, all this time, on our money, Frank.

BEGBIE

My God. Did Renton clock him?

SIMON

No, but Gav followed him. He went into an office block, not far from the centre of town. Gav had to split then, but he's going back next week. He's going to hang out, follow Renton home. And then . . .

BEGBIE

You and me are going to pay him a visit.

                            SIMON
Exactly.

                            BEGBIE
I'll need a passport.

                            SIMON
I can get you one.

                            BEGBIE
I'll take some weapons.

                            SIMON
We can probably get weapons there, Franco.

                            BEGBIE
Aye. Probably. Got most stuff in Amsterdam, haven't they?

                            SIMON
Yes. Now, the important thing for you is to keep your head
down.

                            BEGBIE
Right.

                            SIMON
A low profile till the passport comes through and I get the
tickets. This is an opportunity, Frank.

                            BEGBIE
We will tear him to pieces.

                            SIMON
We most definitely fucking will!

Begbie snarls loud and angry.

Simon joins in.

*Now both of them are making their war faces, raging and thumping
their chests.*

EXT. SCOTTISH GOVERNMENT BUILDING. DAY

*Renton approaches the Scottish Government's large functional,
modern headquarters.*

Simon is waiting. Seems a little nervous, over-friendly.

RENTON

All set?

SIMON

Yes. Fine. Are you OK?

RENTON

Yeah.

SIMON

Sure?

RENTON

Why?

SIMON

Nothing . . .

RENTON

Why? What's happened?

SIMON

Nothing. Nothing's happened. I mean I'm really enjoying us, you know, working together. That's all.

RENTON

Right. Good. So . . .

SIMON

Shall we go in?

INT. SCOTTISH GOVERNMENT, OFFICE. DAY

Renton and Simon face the committee, seven or eight strong.

Outside the window, the Leith docks are visible.

Renton refers to a thick folder on the desk between them – the business plan. There are graphs and projections used earlier in his presentation. Now he is summing up.

RENTON

This is the renovation and conversion of an iconic Leith building. We see it as very much an artisanal bed and breakfast experience. A destination in its own right. Art works by local artists on the walls. Locally sourced fresh food. Outreach projects to inspire youngsters in schools to think outside the box, to instil a belief that: yes, they can. There was a time, this port served thousands of ships from around the globe. Now it can rise again, and we see our business as occupying a central role, both physically and emotionally at the heart of the next wave of regeneration in Leith.

SIMON

Leith 2.1.

RENTON

Exactly.

They look, hopeful, towards the committee, who look back at them with the empty eyes of heartless apparatchiks.

INT. PORT SUNSHINE, UPSTAIRS. NIGHT

The space is in darkness, except for a small pool of bright light over a table in the centre. Spud and Veronika are side by side, hunched over big books of samples on the table.

They turn their way through the pages of patterns, occasionally lingering over one, nodding or shaking heads.

SPUD

I used to steal wallpaper, you see. Sell it on to the middle classes. Used to steal all sorts of stuff, actually, till Mark and I got caught. He got off. I got six months. Still, you find out what you're good at inside. Signatures. That's what I discovered. Anyone's. If I seen it once, I could do it. So when I got out, there was no more shoplifting for me. Chequebook, cheque card. Up to Western Union. Signature. Cash in hand. Up to Swanney's, pay off ma debts and buy some skag. Goldmine, that was, for a while.

VERONIKA

What happened?

SPUD

Debit cards. Chip and pin. E-banking. Billionaires moving money at the touch of a button. No room for an artisan like me any more.

VERONIKA

So what did you do?

SPUD

Back on the pavement. Seven days a week.

VERONIKA

This one? Or this one? I like your stories. You should write them down.

SPUD

Aye? Well, who knows, eh?

He chuckles.

I think this one's warmer. More relaxing.

Veronika smiles.

VERONIKA

Exactly what I was thinking. Tell me: who is this Franco?

SPUD

Franco – oh, Francis Begbie, that man's a good story all right.

VERONIKA

Then perhaps I should start with that one.

INT. SIMON'S FLAT. NIGHT

Renton and Simon are in old-married-couple mode. They are watching a film – could be anything, an old Van Damme movie, a black-and-white classic, a documentary. There are cardboard pizza boxes, bottles of lager.

They converse lazily while watching the film.

SIMON

Doing what?

RENTON

Writing them down.

SIMON

Really?

RENTON

That's what he told me.

SIMON

Murphy?

The mind boggles.

RENTON

Apparently so.

RENTON

Yeah.

SIMON

So who's going to read them?

RENTON

Well, no one can read them at the moment, that's the
problem. That's why he wants me to . . . So he can get a,
you know . . . go with him . . .

He trails off. The movie on the screen plays on.

*Simon's phone rings. He offers a cheerful greeting without checking the
caller.*

SIMON

Hello!

INT. LOCKUP. NIGHT

BEGBIE

What's fucking happening, Simon?

*Begbie is in Mikey Forrester's lockup, on a nest made from boxes of
stolen electrical goods and a couple of old duvets and pillows.*

*One of the televisions has been rigged up with an aerial and the
inevitable* Supercasino *is on.*

INT. SIMON'S FLAT. NIGHT

Simon is out the sofa like he's been ejected, talking loud so as to avoid Begbie's voice spilling out into Renton's hearing, grimacing and smiling towards Renton as if – 'Sorry about this, just have to take this call.'

SIMON

Oh, hello, hold on! Just let me . . .!

He reaches the hallway, where he can see Renton, still absorbed in the film he is watching.

SIMON

Sorry about that. Women. You know.

INT. LOCKUP. NIGHT

Begbie emerges from his nest, paces around the stacks of stolen goods, a caged beast.

Simon is thinking fast: how to best control the beast.

BEGBIE

So have you found the cunt yet?

SIMON

Found him. Exactly.

BEGBIE

Ever since you told me, all I can think about is Renton Renton Renton. I want to kill him, Simon. I want to rip his fucking heart out.

SIMON

I know that, Franco.

BEGBIE

So where the fuck is he?

SIMON

Right now – I don't know.

BEGBIE

Aw fir fuck's sake. I'm cooped up here, Simon. I need to get out there. This is worse than being in fucking prison. If I don't get out soon, I'm going to fucking hurt some cunt.

SIMON

Franco, calm down – let me explain. It's all good.

BEGBIE

Better be –

Simon keeps his eyes on Renton.

SIMON

Gav went back to Amsterdam. Waited outside Renton's
work – no sign of him. So he blagged his way in and asks
around – old mate of mine, etcetera etcetera – turns out
Renton's taken six months off and gone to London.

BEGBIE

Aw fuck –

SIMON

Yeah, but get this – the gadge who spoke to Gav told him
he thought he was only stopping in London a couple of
weeks and after that, Renton was headed for . . . Edinburgh.

A silence at the other end.

Frank?

*He can hear Begbie's breathing. Begbie struggles to absorb the prospect
of revenge so tantalising now. Simon is calm, soothing: the Begbie
whisperer.*

I've got my spies out, Frank, I'll know the moment he
arrives. The main thing now is for you to take no risks and
stay exactly where you are –

BEGBIE

I'm cooped up, Sick Boy!

SIMON

Stoke the anger, Franco . . . And when the time is right . . .
when the time is right –

His eyes are focused on the oblivious Renton.

I will unleash you.

He ends the call. Composes himself. Returns to the sofa.

                          RENTON
All right?

                          SIMON
The ex.

Shakes his head: women . . .

                          RENTON
Yeah.

On television, the movie/documentary plays on.

INT. LOCKUP. NIGHT

Begbie calms himself down. With difficulty. Opens a stolen fridge and cracks open a stolen beer.

But as he reaches for it, he notices something else at the back of the fridge. For Mikey, it appears, fences more than stolen white goods. There are boxes of pills, the boxes are in stacks of twelve or so, held together by clear polythene.

Curious, Begbie lifts one out and rips away the polythene.

He examines the pack in his hand: VIAGRA.

Takes a swig of beer: well, why not . . .

EXT. TOP OF LEITH WALK. DAY

A gleaming glass electronics store.

INT. APPLE STORE. DAY

An enthusiastic, floppy-haired, aesthetically perfect Salesman has been leading them along the products. He delivers his spiel to Renton, who is mainly rolling his eyes at the patter, and to Spud, who nods and agrees, as though he works in the microprocessor industry.

                          SALESMAN
It's really all about finding what's right for you, what feels true to you as a person.

Spud nods sagely.

This: 27 inch, 5K retina, 3 terabyte fusion, 3.7 teraflops of
graphics power, terabyte of flash, 1800 gigs of read-through.
But the real beauty is in the design and in how the design
complements what you bring to it as a human. Sixth gen
Intel quad-core is taken as read. Four gig! You literally
couldn't ask for anything faster. But if you did – you can
always turbo it up: 4.2G's for processor-intensive applications.

SPUD

Of course. Naturally.

SALESMAN

I'm going to leave you . . . to reflect.

*A beat. Renton and Spud try to look like they are reflecting. The
Salesman turns and walks away.*

RENTON

Jesus.

Spud is looking at MacBooks.

SPUD

How about one of these?

RENTON

You can get a laptop for half the price.

SPUD

Or an iPad, man. Nice, eh.

RENTON

Let's go somewhere else –

SPUD

I'd like one of these, man.

*Spud cradles the iPad. His fingers close around the security lead
plugged into it.*

Renton suddenly realises what Spud is planning.

RENTON

No. No, Spud, no . . . That's really not a good idea.

SPUD

Let's do it.

RENTON

I'm not involved in this.

SPUD

You're ma accomplice, Mark.

He thrusts the iPad into Renton's hands.

RENTON

Daniel – we are not doing this.

SPUD

Since when is it 'Daniel'?

RENTON

We are not doing this.

A beat. Stand-off.

Then – with the iPad still in Renton's hands – Spud yanks out the security cable. Looks at Renton with insolent defiance.

Alarms start.

RENTON

Fuck.

He tosses the iPad into Spud's hands. Spud throws it back to him. Back and forth it goes as the Security work out which alarm has been triggered.

EXT. LEITH WALK DAY

Renton and Spud flee down Leith Walk. They are at first pursued by a couple of Security Guards but they outrun them . . .

EXT. OLD TRAMSHED. DAY

The same place where the young boys were playing football at the start, only even more derelict and vandalised now.

Renton and Spud take refuge, catching their breath. They got away.

RENTON

Where is it?

SPUD

I dropped it.

Both laugh.

RENTON

Have to go back then, won't we?

Then a solemnity creeps over them.

SPUD

D'you remember, Mark? Days gone by and that.

Renton thinks. There's an old football. He kicks it hard and it smacks against the brickwork.

EXT. CORROUR STATION. DAY

The train pulls away.

Three figures against the bleak vast landscape. The middle of nowhere.

Spud lifts out a sheet of printed A4. He looks at it briefly, then hands it to Renton. Renton reads aloud.

RENTON

'Tommy looks well. It's terrifying. He's gaunny die. Sometime between the next few weeks and next fifteen years, Tommy will be no more. The chances are that ah'll be exactly the same. The difference is we ken this wi' Tommy . . . Tommy cannot get oot. He cannae afford to heat this gaff, put hissel in a bubble, live in the warm, eat good fresh food, keep his mind stimulated with new challenges. He willnae live five or ten or fifteen years before he is crushed by pneumonia or cancer. Tommy will not survive winter in West Granton.'

He hands the sheet back to Spud who folds it up then walks away, across the heather.

Renton and Simon stand in silence for a beat.

SIMON

I'm trying hard, Mark, but I'm not feeling anything. We were young, bad things happened. It's over. Can we go home now?

RENTON

Two hours till the next train.

SIMON

Fuck's sake.

RENTON

We are here as an act of memorial.

SIMON

Nostalgia. That's why you're here, Mark. A tourist in your own youth. Just because you had a near-death experience and now you're feeling all fuzzy and warm. An innocent stroll down the byways of your own memory. What other little moments will you be revisiting? Here's a good one: how about the time you sold Tommy his very first hit, leading him on to heroin addiction, HIV infection and, ultimately, his death at the age of what was it, twenty-two, twenty-three?

RENTON

Twenty-two.

SIMON

And how innocent was that?

RENTON

That's mine. How's yours?

SIMON

Don't know what you're talking about.

RENTON

She'd be a woman now. Maybe kids of her own. But she never got that far, did she, never got to lead her life because her father, someone who should have been looking after her, protecting his infant, was too busy filling his own veins with heroin to notice that she wasn't breathing properly. How d'you keep the lid on that one?

Simon says nothing.

INT. SPUD'S BEDSIT. NIGHT

Renton and Simon take heroin.

They say nothing.

The needle, the spoon, the powder, the lemon juice.

The hit. The rush washes over Renton, then Simon.

The moment plays out in its own time.

From a far corner, attracted and repulsed in equal measure, just managing to hold himself back but unable to tear his eyes away, Spud watches.

And afterwards. When the thrill has gone and the dust has settled.

> RENTON
>
> Well, that's that.

INT. LOCKUP. NIGHT

Begbie is preparing for a night out.

A liberal spray of Lynx. Trim the moustache.

Pops a Viagra. Another for luck.

A classic 1980s track bleeds in . . .

EXT. CLUB. NIGHT

The classic 1980s track is getting louder.

A taxi pulls up.

Renton and Simon get out.

INT. VERONIKA'S APARTMENT BLOCK. NIGHT

Spud ascends the stairs, an A4 envelope in his hand. He reaches a door – Veronika's. He pauses, deciding, then slips the envelope under the door.

INT. CLUB. NIGHT

It is a 1980s night. A packed big dance floor. An older crowd.

Renton and Simon, up dancing. Simon is shouting in the ear of a thirty-year-old woman.

INT. CLUB. NIGHT

A taxi pulls up.

Begbie gets out. The 1980s incarnate. Jumper tucked into his trousers. Plus the hat and shades as before.

INT. CLUB ENTRANCE. NIGHT

Begbie passes the kiosk and enters the club.

INT. CLUB. NIGHT

Simon is still out there on the dance floor somewhere.

But Renton has had enough, the novelty worn thin. He finishes his drink. Toys with the idea of another but thinks better of it.

INT. VERONIKA'S APARTMENT. NIGHT

Veronika enters her bedsit. As she closes the door, she notices the envelope and picks it up.

She opens it, lifts out the few pages of manuscript inside. She is pleased, curious to read.

INT. CLUB. NIGHT

Begbie buys a drink for a Woman who seems to be enjoying his attention.

> BEGBIE
>
> There you go, doll.

> WOMAN
>
> Cheers.

I'm just off for a slash. Back in a mo and we'll see what's happening, eh?

INT. TOILET CUBICLE I. NIGHT

Nightclub music audible. Renton kicks the lid down and sits on the toilet.

He digs out his phone. He deliberates, then dials.

INT. VERONIKA'S APARTMENT . NIGHT

Veronika sits with the pages in her hand, reading.

Her phone rings. She looks at the caller . . . at the story in her hand . . . Which will it be . . . ? She rejects the call.

INT. TOILET CUBICLE I. NIGHT

Renton hears Veronika's voicemail greeting. He contemplates leaving a message, but unsure what to say, he hangs up.

He sits for a beat, thinking.

Then his reverie is broken as someone noisily enters the adjacent cubicle, sings along to the nightclub music while taking a noisy piss.

INT. TOILET CUBICLE 2. NIGHT

Begbie, excited, fidgety, sits down on the pan and gets a packet of Viagra out.

Fumbles.

The strip of Viagra falls.

He tries to catch it with his foot but succeeds only in kicking it under the partition into cubicle 1.

INT. TOILET CUBICLE 1. NIGHT

Renton notices the strip of Viagra.

A hand is vainly reaching under the partition. Tattoos and sovies.

Renton smiles and picks up the strip.

> RENTON
> What's all this then? Planning a special event, are we, sir?

INT. TOILET CUBICLE 2. NIGHT

> BEGBIE
> Just gie us the fucking tablets, pal.

He snaps his fingers under the partition, demanding them back.

INT. TOILET CUBICLE 1. NIGHT

> RENTON
> Remember not to exceed the stated dose.

INT. TOILET CUBICLE 2. NIGHT

> BEGBIE
> Give me those fucking tablets before I come round and pan
> your fucking head in.

INT. TOILET CUBICLE 1. NIGHT

> RENTON
> OK, calm down.

He passes the Viagra under the partition and the strip of pills is snatched up.

INT. TOILET CUBICLES 1 AND 2. NIGHT

Both toilets in one frame.

Begbie squeezes a pill out and is about to take it, but something stops him.

Renton contemplates redialling, then something stops him.

It takes a while for both to compute their recognition of each other's voices.

Silence.

Both men stand up.

INT. VERONIKA'S APARTMENT. NIGHT

Veronika reads the manuscript.

> VERONIKA
> (*voice-over*)
> 'Renton looked at the bag full of cash, the first time Begbie has let it out of his sight.'

INT. TOILET CUBICLES 1 AND 2. NIGHT

The two men poised as before, each man's movements incredibly slow, deliberate and silent.

> VERONIKA
> (*voice-over*)
> 'Renton has never seen so much money. He empties it from Begbie's bag and stuffs it into his own. He turns and scuttles from the room. If he meets Begbie now, he is dead. As soon as that thought forms in his mind, he nearly collapses with fear. But he meets no one and he crosses the road. He has escaped, and he can never go back.'

Begbie dips his hand inside his jacket. It emerges complete with brass knuckle.

Renton's hand slowly slowly reaches out to catch on the door.

When he flicks it, it's as loud as the starter's pistol.

INT. CLUB ENTRANCE. NIGHT

Simon is standing, looking around.

He is knocked aside by Renton flying for the exit.

He picks himself up.

A moment later he is knocked aside again by Begbie in hot pursuit.

EXT. EDINBURGH STREETS. NIGHT

Chase. Life or death. Renton's fuel: total fear. Begbie's fuel: total hate.

They exit the club under the North Bridge . . . up the stone steps to the North Bridge . . . across the High Street . . . down one narrow close . . . then up another . . . then back downhill and through the Grassmarket revellers

Renton keeping ahead but not losing Begbie at all.

Renton reaches the Castle Terrace multi-storey car park.

EXT. MULTI-STOREY CAR PARK. NIGHT

In the depths of the multi-storey. Half full. Begbie stops.

Renton is here. Nearby. Hiding behind one of the cars. Begbie can sense it.

But which one?

A man approaches from the distance, walking towards Begbie. Begbie glares at the Man who avoids catching Begbie's eye. The man walks on to a 4WD with roof bars.

EXT. CLUB ENTRANCE. NIGHT

Standing just outside the club, Simon dials on his mobile.

EXT. MULTI-STOREY CAR PARK. NIGHT

Behind a car:

Renton – his mobile rings.

RENTON

Fuck!

Begbie spins around, locks on to the sound before Renton can silence it.

EXT. CLUB ENTRANCE. NIGHT

> SIMON
> Rentboy – Where the – Mark? Shit.

EXT. MULTI-STOREY CAR PARK. NIGHT

Renton stands against the wall, behind a car.

Begbie stands in the centre of the driveway. They face each other.

The 4WD moves out of its parking space.

Renton runs towards it, away from Begbie. He throws himself on to the roof. Holds on to the bars.

Begbie draws a knife from his jacket.

INT. FOUR-WHEEL DRIVE. NIGHT

The Man, terrified by Renton's apparent assault and Begbie ahead with the knife, slams his foot to the floor.

EXT. MULTI-STOREY CAR PARK. NIGHT

The 4WD accelerates past Begbie with Renton clinging to the roof.

Begbie slashes at Renton. The sharp blade slices along the length of his arm from his hand up towards his shoulder.

Renton holds on, blood already flowing.

The vehicle screams away.

Begbie curses.

EXT. MULTI-STOREY CAR PARK, EXIT. NIGHT. / INT. 4WD. NIGHT

At the barrier, the 4WD stops.

Renton slithers off, leaving a trail of blood down the windscreen.

The Man activates the wipers and the screenwash. The blood is smeared, then washed away.

Renton has gone. The street ahead is empty.

INT. HOSPITAL A&E. DAY

The long wound on Renton's arm is stitched. Renton is glazed, traumatised as he inhales deeply from a cylinder of Entenox.

INT. DIANE'S CAR. DAY / EXT. EDINBURGH. DAY

Diane drives Renton away from the hospital. Renton is chastened, and scared – fearing Begbie might appear from anywhere. He slumps down in the seat, eyeing the world beyond with suspicion.

Diane is silently scornful. The unspoken comment: at your age.

INT. HOTEL ROOM. DAY

Renton's room. He isn't there, but Diane is, briskly, contemptuously even, packing his clothes into his small suitcase.

INT. DIANE'S HOME. DAY

The front door opens and Diane leads Renton in, the latter at last relieved to be in what feels like a place of safety.

Diane indicates a door that leads through to a small spare room.

Renton turns to say something, but he can see she isn't in the mood. He goes into the room.

Diane stands for a beat, exasperated, conflicted. She walks away.

EXT. EDINBURGH. DAY

Simon sits on a bench at the edge of a park. Looking this way and that, he does not hear Renton approach.

> RENTON
> Brought him with you, have you?

> SIMON
> I didn't know.

Renton glares at him. There is no question of believing a single word of Simon's bullshit.

SIMON

OK . . . OK . . . I may have, you know . . . heard something.
I'm sorry I didn't mention it –

RENTON

May have heard something!

SIMON

All right – fuck it, I knew! I knew he was out. And I could
have served you up to him on a plate any time I wanted to!

RENTON

And I'm sure you were going to!

SIMON

Yes! Yes, I was! I was looking forward to it!

RENTON

I ought to fucking kill you.

*They sit in hostile silence, each inwardly deciding whether to kiss or
kill the other. Ahead of them, a shiny people-carrier pulls up. They
don't anticipate that it is anything to do with them.*

*The door slides open and a hard-looking man gets out. He walks
casually up to them. Stops right in front of them.*

HARD MAN

Get in the car.

INT. CAR. DUSK. / EXT. AI, EAST LOTHIAN. DUSK

*Renton and Simon sit in the middle seats. There's the hard-looking
guy driving, and another one behind them. In the front passenger seat
is the Capo: Doyle.*

No one says a word.

*They are driven in silence out along the AI and then along winding
roads through the countryside of East Lothian.*

EXT. FOREST. NIGHT

*Simon and Renton stand, illuminated by the vehicle lights, at the end
of a forest track.*

The two hard men stand back while Doyle takes a look at his two prisoners. Eventually, he addresses them.

DOYLE

So, it's Mark, right? And Simon . . . You know who I am? Good. And you know that I own several saunas on the north side of Edinburgh. In fact I own all the saunas on the north side of Edinburgh. So your little venture was never going to happen. It couldn't. I couldn't have you, on my doorstep, in competition for my clients, for my employees. No, that could never happen, could it?

Renton says nothing.

SIMON

No, Mr Doyle.

Renton flashes a contemptuous glance at Simon.

DOYLE

No. That's the right answer, Simon. It couldn't, and it's not going to. Right?

Simon nods.

Doyle pauses. Contemplates them.

Well, I've done my due diligence, and as I understand it you are no threat to me. Which is good news for all of us. A couple of losers: that's what I've been told. A couple of losers. What do you think of that, Simon?

SIMON

Probably right enough, Mr Doyle.

DOYLE

Aye. Probably right enough.

He stares at each of them, saying nothing. Memorising their faces, deciding their fate.

The interview is over. He walks back to the car and gets in.

The two hard men approach and stand opposite Renton and Simon. It isn't clear what happens now. This could be their last seconds on earth.

Take your clothes off.

EXT. EAST LOTHIAN. DAWN

*In the wide flat empty fields of East Lothian. Rich ploughed earth.
A copse on the horizon. Not a soul to be seen.*

*Suddenly two figures silhouetted on the skyline flit across the ploughed
landscape making the dash from copse to hedgerow.*

EXT. HEDGEROW. DAWN

*Renton and Simon crouch naked in the hedgerow, just two white arses
and a bundle of shame.*

Now they have a road to cross.

There is a farmhouse not far away.

> RENTON
'Probably right enough, Mr Doyle.'

> SIMON
If you'd grovelled a bit more, we might not be going home
in the buff.

> RENTON
At least I have my dignity.

> SIMON
That what you're calling it?

> RENTON
Are you ready?

> SIMON
Yeah.

> RENTON
Let's go!

EXT. FARMHOUSE. DAWN

The two naked figures run through the farmyard, emerging with scraps of hessian sack hastily wrapped about themselves.

INT. APARTMENT BLOCK. DAY

The buzzer is pressed at a door.

Veronika opens it.

She finds herself facing Renton and Simon, dressed in the hessian, along with other scraps of clothing that they have scavenged along the way. Renton has one tattered shoe on, toe flapping open like a caricature tramp. Otherwise nothing on their feet but mud.

She contemplates the two bedraggled, exhausted, miserable, desperate and wholly unattractive men in front of her.

INT. VERONIKA'S APARTMENT. DAY

Renton and Simon have showered now and put on some fresh clothes, except that they belong to Veronika.

Renton is wearing a shorty towelling bathrobe while Simon is in a girl's baggy T-shirt. Neither is a flattering look. They sit side by side.

They are both still so miserable, they hardly notice that Veronika is struggling to suppress her amusement as she serves them coffee.

She sits opposite them. Slowly, she unbuttons her blouse and leans forward.

                    VERONIKA
Hello, boys!

She starts laughing, buttoning up again.

The 'boys' are not amused. Head in hands. Eyes closed. Too preoccupied with their misfortune.

                    SIMON
What is so funny?

She takes a photograph with her phone.

SIMON

Delete that right now!

VERONIKA

I put it on Twitter. No one will see.

SIMON

Veronika – don't you understand! There isn't going to be a sauna. Never. It's over.

VERONIKA

I know that.

SIMON

We have lost everything!

VERONIKA

Did you not see the email?

SIMON

No, because owing to an encounter with some violent and threatening criminals, we simply haven't got round to –

VERONIKA

We got the money.

SIMON

What?

RENTON

How much?

VERONIKA

The money. The – what do you call it – small business development –

RENTON

HOW MUCH!

VERONIKA

Fifty thousand pounds.

A supernova explosion of joy, hugging, kissing, loving.

INT. BEDSIT BLOCK. DAY

Spud climbs the steps, carrying a bag of groceries. He reaches his door. He notices that the lock is burst again.

He steps inside cautiously.

INT. SPUD'S BEDSIT. DAY

As Spud steps in, a voice.

> BEGBIE
>
> Hello, Murphy.

Spud freezes. Struck dumb. Can manage only to say:

> SPUD
>
> Franco?

> BEGBIE
>
> Sit down.

Spud hesitates.

> Sit down.

Spud complies.

> Now where is he?

Spud is about to speak.

> And don't say 'Who?' Don't say 'I don't know'. Just tell me where he is.

Silence. Begbie waits.

> You still a junky, Murphy?

> SPUD
>
> I'm clean, Franco.

> BEGBIE
>
> You? Clean? Fucking joke. Got any Beck's?

> SPUD
>
> I, eh . . . don't drink, Franco.

BEGBIE

What cunt disnae drink? You must've fuckin' something.

He begins randomly searching.

Now where is he, anyway?

SPUD

I don't know.

Begbie spins around, eyes blazing.

BEGBIE

DON'T SAY THAT!

This could be the end. Then something catches Begbie's eye. A thick pile of printed A4: the manuscript.

BEGBIE

What is this?

He picks up some pages.

SPUD

I was just . . . Stories.

BEGBIE

Stories? What are you writing stories for, Murphy? Who's going to read shite written by a cunt like you?

SPUD

It was just for . . . likesay, my granchildren, ken.

BEGBIE

Have you got grandchildren?

SPUD

No –

BEGBIE

Well, what are you fucking well writing stories for them? Maybe they'll no' like stories. Eh? Had you no' thought of that?

SPUD

Aye, s'pose you're right enough there, Franco.

Begbie reads.

BEGBIE

'The sweat wis lashing oafay Sick Boy . . . The sweat
wis . . .' Sick Boy? Is it about him?

SPUD

Well . . . all of us, likes –

BEGBIE

All of us! Me!

He starts furiously rifling through the pages.

SPUD

No, no' you, Frank –

BEGBIE

Better no' be . . . Hold on, what is this? 'Strolling Through
the Meadows' . . . Read!

He thrusts the page towards Spud.

SPUD

What?

BEGBIE

Read it!

Spud takes it. He begins, in a halting, frightened voice.

SPUD

'The pub's, likesay, dead busy, full eh loco-locals and
festival types, having a wee snort before heading off to the
next show. And Begbie's . . . Begbie's . . .' I was going to cut
this bit out, Frank.

BEGBIE

Read!

SPUD

'Begbie's pished his jeans.'

Spud closes his eyes, braced for the fatal impact.

Begbie's face looks grim, when suddenly he breaks into a smile.

BEGBIE

I remember that night!

SPUD

Huh!

BEGBIE

Read on, read on!

INT. GASTROPUB. DAY

The pastries are ignored this time.

Renton watches Veronika closely, awaiting some response, but slowly, slowly, she stirs her coffee.

Eventually, he feels the need to add more.

RENTON

Simon knew that Frank Begbie was out, but he chose to keep that secret, and I owe him nothing.

She looks up. Their eyes meet.

INT. SPUD'S BEDSIT. DAY

Spud continues reading, Begbie hanging on his every word, acting it out with a knife as the memories flood back.

SPUD

'Begbie went fucking crazy, got likesay that carried away with the bladework, ken, we nearly forgot the wallet, likes. Blood was flowin' intae the latrine and mixin' with the pish . . .'

BEGBIE

Read that bit again.

SPUD

'The blood was flowin' intae the latrine and mixin' with the pish.'

BEGBIE

Blood mixin' with the pish!

'Ugly, man.'

Begbie is searching the manuscript for more.

BEGBIE
Murphy, you have hidden talents.

INT. SIMON'S FLAT. DAY

Simon addresses Veronika. The flat has been tidied up. More than that, transformed. Everything is sorted, neat, and clean. Simon watches Veronika progress around it, notes her astonished smile, sees her run her finger along a surface, not a speck of dust.

SIMON
Mark stole from me, his best friend. And this moment has been a long time coming.

She looks at him.

INT. SPUD'S BEDSIT. DAY

Spud reads from another page to his eager audience of one.

From 'A Glass'.

As Spud reads, Begbie, locked into memory, mimes throwing the glass over his shoulder.

SPUD
'All ah did wis put a pint of export in front of Begbie. He takes one fuckin' gulp out ay it; then he throws the empty glass from his last pint straight over the balcony, in a casual, backhand motion. Ah look at Begbie, whae smiles. The glass crashes doon on this girl's heid, which splits open as she faws to her knees. Begbie's on his feet 'n racing doon the stair and he shouts –'

Begbie – without reading from the page – recalls his own declaration that famous night.

'The lassie got glassed and no cunt leaves here till we find out what cunt did it!'

INT. GASTROPUB. DAY

Renton and Simon sit opposite one another with drinks.

RENTON

That was a long time ago.

SIMON

Yes. It was. And I forgive you.

A beat. They remember. They look at one another.

You know, in the morning, when you were gone – with my money – I was furious . . . but also, I thought . . . of course, he's taken it. Why wouldn't he?

INT. SPUD'S BEDSIT. DUSK

Begbie is still locked into the reverie of his last reminiscence.

He repeats the line softly to himself, pondering its meanings, thinking of all the fates intertwined in a single moment.

BEGBIE

'And no cunt leaves here till we find out what cunt did it.'

He comes out of it.

That's lovely. What else you got?

He picks up another page. Skim-reading, his face clouds: puzzled, angry.

What's this? London? . . . 'Renton had never seen so much money . . . He stole the money, took it from his friends . . .'

He snatches the next page.

SPUD

I made it up, Franco.

'Renton felt no sympathy for Begbie. No, Renton's real guilt centred round Spud. He loved Spud. Spud had never hurt anybody. If there was one person whom Renton would try to compensate, it was Spud.'

It's all too clear now.

Compensate.

Begbie is calm.

BEGBIE

I'm only going to ask you once: how much money did he leave for you?

SPUD

Four thousand pounds. Left it in a locker.

BEGBIE

You didn't mention that at the time, Spud.

SPUD

Sorry, Franco.

Long pause.

BEGBIE

I need a drink.

EXT. SPUD'S BEDSIT. DUSK

Begbie walks away from the block.

INT. SPUD'S BEDSIT. NIGHT

Spud is trussed up with cable ties and thick gaffer tape. He's going nowhere.

INT. PUB. NIGHT

Begbie sits at the bar: a nip and a pint. Thinking deeply about the extent of the betrayal. He finishes the pint, gestures to the Barman.

Another shot.

On the bar in front of him is the creased page from Spud's manuscript.
He looks at it again.

> BEGBIE
> (*voice-over*)
> 'Renton felt no sympathy for Begbie . . .'

He slugs back the shot. He folds away the sheet of paper.

INT. SPUD'S BEDSIT. NIGHT

Spud tied up as before. But he hears someone outside.

A knock on the door. A voice.

> VERONIKA
> (*out of shot*)
> Daniel? . . . Daniel – it's me.

Spud wriggles, and shouts through the muffling tape.

Veronika pushes the door – its lock broken – gently open.

> VERONIKA
> Daniel – are you in there? Oh my God!

Shocked by what she finds, she has the presence of mind to help him.
Quickly she finds a knife, in Begbie's kit, and cuts him free. Helps him
to the bed. A drink of water. A damp cloth to wipe his face.

> VERONIKA
> Oh Daniel, who did this?

> SPUD
> We better get out of here –

> VERONIKA
> What is happening?

> SPUD
> He'll be back any moment!

> VERONIKA
> Who will?

And the door is kicked open again.

Begbie takes in the scene. Veronika and Spud freeze.

BEGBIE

Well, well, well. Rescue! This your bird, Murphy?

SPUD

Please, Franco, leave her alone, she's got nothing to do with this.

BEGBIE

Has now.

He approaches Veronika. She backs away until she reaches the wall and can back no further.

He sniffs her neck. He takes his time, very suspicious, working it all out as he goes along.

BEGBIE

What's your name, doll?

VERONIKA

Veronika.

BEGBIE

Veronika. Lovely. And how did you chum up with Mr Murphy here?

VERONIKA

Simon –

BEGBIE

Simon! Good old Simon! . . . And how about Simon's very best friend? Ken him and all?

He catches the glance between Spud and Veronika – confirms his suspicion.

You got a phone?

VERONIKA

A phone?

BEGBIE

A mobile phone. Yes. You know the sort of thing –

                    VERONIKA
    Yes –

                    BEGBIE
    Give it to me.

She stares him in the eyes.

                    VERONIKA
    You have to let us live. Both of us.

A fraction of a gesture from Begbie.

She gives him the phone.

INT. GASTROPUB. NIGHT

Renton and Simon drink.

                    SIMON
    Another?

                    RENTON
    I'm fine.

On the table Simon's phone buzzes with a text. Renton glances towards it but Simon makes no move to read it.

A beat later, Renton's phone does the same. Simon glances at it but Renton makes no move to read it.

INT. SPUD'S BEDSIT. NIGHT

Begbie slips the phone away, back into his pocket.

He is calm. His moment is coming.

EXT. BEDSIT BLOCK. NIGHT

Veronika hurries away from the block to where Spud is waiting for her.

                    SPUD
    You all right?

She nods. They are relieved, still shaken by the experience, the narrow escape from harm.

A thought strikes him.

                              SPUD
     Veronika – what did you come round for in the first place?

She turns to him.

                            VERONIKA
     Because I have an idea for you.

INT. DIANE'S HOME, KITCHEN. NIGHT

*Early evening. Diane is at the hob, cooking, when Renton appears in
the doorway.*

                             RENTON
     Diane – I thought I should let you know I probably won't
     be staying much longer.

She barely turns.

                             DIANE
     Right. OK.

                             RENTON
     In fact I might be going tonight.

                             DIANE
     If you just leave the key on the table.

                             RENTON
     Don't you want to know where I'm going?

She looks at him for a beat.

                             DIANE
     You know, she really is too young for you.

                             RENTON
     Who says it's got anything to do with her?

Even he doesn't expect her to believe that. She waits him out.

     I didn't ask for your opinion.

                             DIANE
     So why are you telling me?

RENTON

I don't know. I just . . .

Why did I tell her?

Because I was hoping you would stop me.

DIANE

I'm not stopping you. I'm not here for that. I'll solve your problems and I'll pick up the pieces and bring you in out of the cold, but I'm not going to stop you making a fool of yourself. That's up to you.

RENTON

Do you ever wonder –

DIANE

No. I don't.

RENTON

I do. If you and me . . . if things had been different . . .

DIANE

No, Mark: if you'd been different.

INT. SPUD'S BEDSIT. NIGHT

Begbie, alone. Waiting. Checks his watch. Still some time to kill. He picks up another sheet of manuscript and reads.

BEGBIE
(*voice-over*)
'We go for a pish in the old Central Station.'

INT. DISUSED RAILWAY STATION. NIGHT

A Victorian hangar, now dilapidated and dark. Empty. The sound of pigeons fluttering in the dark.

Renton and Begbie are just visible, in and out of stray beams of moonlight.

BEGBIE
(*voice-over*)
The place is empty, soon to be demolished.

RENTON

Some size ay a station this was. Used to be steam engines to all over from here, or so they say.

BEGBIE
(*voice-over*)

An old drunkard, whom Begbie had been looking at, lurched up tae us, wine boatil in his hand.

WINO

What yis up to, lads?

BEGBIE
(*voice-over*)

He sais . . . 'What yis up to?'

WINO

Trainspotting in Leith Central?

BEGBIE
(*voice-over*)

He sais, laughing. He staggered oaf. His rasping, drunkard's cackles filling the desolate barn. Ah noticed Begbie seemed strangely subdued and uncomfortable. It was only then ah realised that the auld wino wis Begbie's faither.'

INT. SPUD'S BEDSIT. NIGHT

Begbie stares at the sheet of type in his hand.

INT. VERONIKA'S APARTMENT. NIGHT

The blinds are drawn. Spud sits at the table in the only light. Hovering around him, intimidating and persuasive, is Veronika. There is a sheet of paper on the table but we don't see what, if anything, is on it. Spud wants to hear the Siren, but not sure if he can resist.

VERONIKA

First, there is an opportunity, and then there is a betrayal. And that's how it ends.

SPUD

I think I already wrote that one.

VERONIKA

Yes, Daniel, but *this* one, this one needs an ending too.

She holds out a pen.

Spud looks at the pen. It is waiting for him.

EXT. BEGBIE FAMILY HOME. NIGHT

A buzzing at the door. June opens it. She is terrified to see Begbie on the landing.

Begbie sees his son in the hallway behind her. He nods to each and speaks respectfully.

BEGBIE

June. Frank Junior . . . Could I come in for a moment?

INT. BEGBIE FAMILY HOME. NIGHT

The mother and son sit, still frightened, facing Begbie.

BEGBIE

I'm going away. One way or another, be a long time before you see me again.

They're really not sure what they're supposed to say to that. So they say nothing.

And ah . . . ah just thought I'd come by . . .

This is difficult for him, but it's from the heart.

Just thought I'd come by and wish you good luck, son. That's all.

A moment of stunned silence.

FRANK JUNIOR

Uh . . . uh . . . thanks, Dad.

See . . . It's difficult for me, cos we didnae have aw that when ah was a boy.

They don't know what he's talking about.

That likesay Hotel . . .

Management.

Aye. Hotel fucking Management. Aw that shite and that. Never had any of that. Still. World changes, eh, June?

She nods timorously. He smiles at her.

Even if we don't, eh?

She sort of smiles too, through the tear that is welling up as he squeezes her hand.

So you . . . you look after yourself, son.

He stands. Frank Junior snaps to his feet too.

The auld wino wis my faither. And this fool is yours.

Begbie extends a stiff hand. Frank Junior takes it.

Begbie's words come from somewhere he has no control of.

But you will be a better man than either of us.

And as he hugs his son, there is a definite moistness across his eyes too.

EXT. EDINBURGH AIRPORT. NIGHT

Veronika approaches the check-in with a single suitcase.

EXT. PORT SUNSHINE. NIGHT

Simon approaches. No one around. He slips in.

INT. PORT SUNSHINE, UPSTAIRS. NIGHT

In the shadows, Simon ascends the narrow stair. He steps cautiously into the darkness.

A light flicks on. The worklight on its extension lead.

> RENTON
>
> She isn't here.

Simon turns, astonished to see Renton.

> SIMON
>
> Mark – what the fuck –?

> RENTON
>
> And my guess is that since we both are, she won't be turning up any time soon.

> SIMON
>
> What?

> RENTON
>
> Veronika and I were going off together. To elope. You understand? To leave you behind.

> SIMON
>
> And what else – rip me off? Steal from me? Is that it?

> RENTON
>
> Yes. And you?

Simon thinks it over. The truth bends him . . .

> SIMON
>
> The same.

A beat.

> So where is she then?

> RENTON
>
> She's gone.

> SIMON
>
> I'm going to call her.

RENTON

It's switched off.

SIMON

And what are we doing here?

RENTON

Her way of saying goodbye, I suppose.

Simon has had the fight knocked out of him. One setback too many.

SIMON

I loved her.

Renton retains a dispassionate calm.

Then suddenly, from below, the sound of a door being flung open.

Simon's face snaps up, beaming with hope.

SIMON

Veronika?

The sound of footsteps. The door facing them swings open.

SPUD

Guys – I'm sorry.

SIMON

I loved that woman!

RENTON

Sorry for what?

Spud freezes – it's a painful confession.

SIMON

Yeah – sorry for what?

SPUD

I shouldn't have . . . But well . . . When she mentioned Ali
and wee Fergus – of course he's not so wee now, I know
that, but still –

SIMON

What are you talking about, Murphy?

Spud hesitates again, gathering his thoughts.

A voice speaks as its owner steps in, emerging from the shadows in the doorway. They never heard him climb the stairs.

BEGBIE

Carry on, Spud.

The moment of shock. No one moves. He drops his bag of kit to the floor, paces around the frozen trio.

We're all dying to hear it.

A beat. Spud – nervous, no choice – continues as ordered.

SPUD

First there is an opportunity, and then there is a betrayal. And that's how it ends.

BEGBIE

We've aw heard that one before, eh Mark?

RENTON

Maybe.

BEGBIE

Aye: maybe.

SIMON

Franco –

BEGBIE

Shut up. Carry on. 'First, there is an opportunity, and then there is a betrayal.'

SPUD

Twenty years have gone by. They got lucky, made some money. Wi' a . . .

BEGBIE

Wi' a hoor fae Bulgaria.

SPUD

Aye.

BEGBIE

It's all right. It's the character talking, no' you.

SPUD

And she puts it to Spud . . .

INT. VERONIKA'S APARTMENT. DAY

The moment when the pen is on offer.

VERONIKA

It will be safe, if you leave with me.

SPUD

But ah cannae go –

(*Voice-over.*) He says, unconvincingly –

I'm likesay the last of the indigenous cats around here.

(*Voice-over.*) Clinging to the hope that he will not commit this crime against his friends.

INT. PORT SUNSHINE, UPSTAIRS. NIGHT

BEGBIE

But she's smart, eh? Got you where she wants you. What did you do, Murphy?

SPUD

She says . . .

INT. VERONIKA'S APARTMENT. DAY

VERONIKA

I'll send you your share.

SPUD

No – I'd just end up back on the skag, man!

VERONIKA

All right – I will send it to Gail, and Fergus.

SPUD
(*voice-over*)
Gail and Fergus. His wife, his son.

The moment.

He takes the pen. And with his gift of forgery, so lately
underused, he signs their names, he transfers the full
£50,000 to a bank in Sofia, Bulgaria.

He signs the bank form in front of him:

Simon Williamson.

Mark Renton.

VERONIKA
Thank you, Daniel.

SPUD
Spud. Most folks call me Spud.

INT. PORT SUNSHINE, UPSTAIRS. NIGHT

Renton and Simon, momentarily forgetting Begbie, are shocked.

BEGBIE
'Last of the indigenous cats.'

SPUD
Sorry, Mark.

RENTON
It's all right, Spud.

SIMON
All right! It is not at all *all right*, Mark!

BEGBIE
Not quite over yet, though, is it?

SPUD
No.

BEGBIE
So how does it end?

SPUD

In a box, Franco.

He stops at his bag. Selects a couple of weapons/tools.

BEGBIE

Aye, in a box. We're all in a box, aren't we? Just waiting for the lid to come down.

SIMON

Frank, I can explain.

BEGBIE

You knew. Stringing me along, so you were.

Simon is moving towards Begbie, hoping to leave Renton isolated.

SIMON

Honestly, please –

And suddenly Begbie strikes him across the side of the head with a tool he held in his hand.

Simon collapses to the floor, conscious but dazed, groaning softly.

BEGBIE

Deal with you later, Sick Boy. Now, Mark: you and me.

Renton isn't going to waste his time pleading. He sets off to escape. Begbie isn't bothered, knows that he will catch his prey. Renton cannot get to the exit. Instead, while Begbie strolls after him, Renton races up the stairs, desperate for some way to protect himself, some way to escape from this place.

Eventually, locking himself behind one of Spud's flimsy doors, he begins to pull away at the structure of the roof in the hope of breaking out.

Spud stays rooted to the spot, paralysed, transfixed by the unfolding events.

BEGBIE

Twenty years, eh? You done all right. And why not? World's all right for smart cunts. Plenty of opportunities for smart cunts. But what about me? What about men like me? What do I get? All I can take with my bare hands? All I can get with my fists? Is that it for me? You know, I killed a man once – a man who'd done nothing to me – just looked at me the wrong way – at a moment when I was thinking of you. Been thinking of you for twenty years. About how you robbed us. Your best mates. Never get my money back, never get my hope back. But I always promised myself that one day . . . Well, here it is. The day has come.

Renton has almost opened enough space to get out on to the roof. Begbie is at the door, calls in.

Come on, Mark, say something. Not like you to be so shy. And I always thought that you got the best lines.

Renton continues to dismantle the roof above him.

RENTON

Oh, don't put yourself down, Frank, you were always very quotable, back in the day.

BEGBIE

Quotable? That's kind. A little patronising maybe . . .

He prepares to smash the door open.

Inside the small space, Renton pauses.

RENTON

But I do remember . . . my first day at primary school my very first day, and the teacher, she said to me: 'Good morning, Mark. You will sit here, beside Francis.' D'you remember that, Franco?

Both pause, lost in reflection for a beat.

BEGBIE

Aye. Ah mind it well enough.

RENTON

And here we are.

INT. PORT SUNSHINE, UPSTAIRS. NIGHT

For just a moment, in an on–off flash of light, it is the Young Begbie and the Young Renton, either side of the door.

Then suddenly:

INT. PORT SUNSHINE, UPSTAIRS. NIGHT

Renton tries to lift himself out and Begbie smashes the door open.

He grabs Renton by the front of his jacket, hauls him out and faces him for a beat.

BEGBIE

Aye. Here we are.

Then, abruptly, he pushes Renton backwards.

There is an area without boards in the floor behind Renton. He falls back and straight through the plasterboard ceiling below.

He becomes tangled in the chaotic arrangement of electrical cabling laid across that ceiling.

He dangles just below the joists, caught in the web of cabling. The more he struggles, the more entwined he becomes. A length of cable becomes snared around his neck.

Begbie takes his time, slowly descending the stairs and approaching the suspended Renton, who struggles in vain.

We rejoin Spud, lost for words now. Begbie looks him in the eye for a moment, then continues towards the dangling Renton.

Meanwhile (intercut with) Simon regains a sort of consciousness.

He looks round at the violent pursuit going on only yards away.

And at that point –

Begbie has reached Renton, dangling from joists above, completely at his mercy.

They are eye to eye for a beat. Then Begbie begins to pull on Renton, using his weight to drag his victim down and the cable noose around his neck draws tighter and tighter.

Renton struggles to breath, desperately trying with one hand to loosen the garotte.

Begbie drags him down harder and harder. Renton's agonal choking is the only sound, when suddenly:

HIIISSSSS!

Begbie screams. Blinded by the jet of CS gas from Simon's canister.

Simon stands back – actually amazed at how effective it was – poised to spray again. Feeling confident, he tries to follow up with another dose – but the canister is empty.

Begbie lashes out – stumbles – rubbing his weeping eyes.

Renton hanging. Simon and Spud staying clear. All eyes on Begbie.

Begbie stumbles – trips over his kit bag. He gasps – instinctively his hands dive into the bag. He feels the barrels of his shotgun and whips it out as his fingers feel around the bag – he's found a cartridge and breaks the gun open, squinting at it as he slots the cartridge home and snaps the gun closed.

He looks up. In front of him, in the dazzled blur he can see the shape of a man hanging from the wires.

Still kneeling on the floor Begbie raises the gun, when –

THUD!

White ceramic smashes hard against the back of his head and Begbie falls to the floor.

Simon helps Renton – unlooping the coil around his neck. Renton falls to the floor then stands.

They look towards their saviour: Spud. He stands there – a toilet in his hands. Trembling, he drops it to the floor.

Now the three men gather and stand in silence to look down at the motionless form of Frank Begbie, a pool of blood forming beside his head.

EXT. NEAR PORT SUNSHINE. DAY / INT. SIMON'S CAR. DAY

Simon gets into the driver's seat. Renton is already in, beside him. Spud in the back.

A beat. There is nothing to say.

Renton and Simon look at one another. The feud is over.

Simon starts the car.

EXT. BULGARIAN TOWN. DAY

At the bus station, as the disembarking crowd clears, Veronika is revealed. She is looking ahead, towards an older woman, her mother.

And beside her mother, big-eyed and solemn, is her son, aged three or four.

She approaches, kneels. She takes the boy in her arms. He is cautious at first, struggling to remember this woman, but he responds to her embrace, and a smile of contentment soon spreads from one to the other and back again.

EXT. RENTON FAMILY HOME. DAY

Renton approaches the door. Rings the doorbell.

His father answers. A moment, then unspoken reconciliation.

A hug from father to son.

EXT. GAIL'S HOME. DAY

Spud looks at the house in front of him.

INT. PORT SUNSHINE, BAR. DAY

Simon walks back in. Closes the door behind him. Mournful. Defeated. A long sigh.

He goes to stand behind the bar.

He picks up a towel. A glass. Begins to polish it. Business as usual. The dream was exactly that.

INT. CAR BOOT. DAY

Darkness, but we can tell it's him.

Begbie is cursing, and hammering at the inside surface of the lid with the jack from the spare wheel.

A spark as he flicks on a cigarette lighter to inspect his progress. By the wavering flame, we can see his bloodied face.

The flame goes out. He redoubles his attack on the lid.

EXT. SAUGHTON PRISON. DAY

Where Simon's car is parked, just in front of the gates.

As the occupant of the boot tries to bludgeon his way out, a group of Police Officers stand patiently watching, their vehicles parked nearby, while another approaches with a tool for breaking the lock.

INT. GAIL'S HOME. DAY

Spud and Gail sit opposite one another at the small kitchen table, across their mugs of tea.

Spud's manuscript, neatly stacked, is set to one side.

> GAIL
>
> I thought of a title.

INT. RENTON'S ROOM. DAY

Exactly as he left it before.

Renton sits on the bed. Unshaven. Unkempt. Jacket crumpled and torn. All the scars of the last few weeks, the last few hours, upon his face. A middle-aged man who's been where he shouldn't but done what he had to do.

He looks around him once more. His youth encloses him again. Train wallpaper. The Hibs posters, the football programmes.

The vinyl albums. He stretches out. He flicks through them. Again, he selects one. He gazes for a moment at the cover, which we do not see.

He slides the vinyl from its sleeve and drops it carefully on to the turntable.

He raises the lever – he lowers the stylus to the vinyl.

The crackle and hiss before the track. He inhales deeply. A smile forms upon his lips.

He's earned it now.

This time he lets it run.

The first three beats are like a rush.

Cut to black.

Audio:

The song plays on in the darkness. We're back where we were. Back where we never left.

> 'Here comes Johnny Yen again
> With the liquor and drugs
> And a flesh machine . . .'

T2
Trainspotting

PHOTOGRAPHS FROM THE FILM

Spud on the road to recovery.

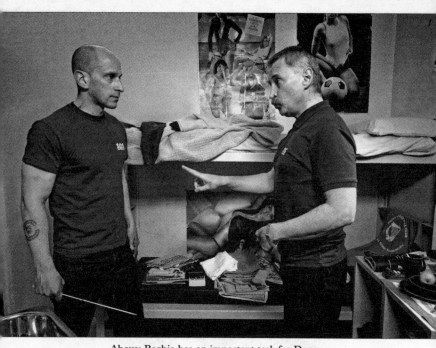

Above: Begbie has an important task for Dozo.

Below: Simon killing time playing pool in Port Sunshine pub.

Above: 'Where have you been, for twenty years?'

Below: Simon stalks a victim.

Above: a father disappointed by his son.
Below: entertaining the Orange Lodge.

Above: Veronika watches Simon's plea to Renton.
Below: Simon's unexpected visitor.

Above: Renton and Begbie, so near yet so far.
Below: two respectable businessmen.

Above: Spud seeks inspriation.

Below: an act of memorial.

Above: taking heroin to forget.

Below: a celebration in Simon's flat.

Above: advice from Diane at an hourly rate.

Below: Begbie recalls the act of betrayal.

Begbie greets his friends in the final act.

Renton listening to Begbie in Port Sunshine pub.